THE SUSAN B. ANTHONY WOMEN'S VOTING RIGHTS TRIAL

A Headline Court Case

Headline Court Cases

THE SUSAN B. ANTHONY WOMEN'S VOTING RIGHTS TRIAL

A Headline Court Case

Judy Monroe

Enslow Publishers, Inc.

40 Industrial Road   PO Box 38
Box 398   Aldershot
Berkeley Heights, NJ 07922   Hants GU12 6BP
USA   UK

http://www.enslow.com

Library of Congress Cataloging-in-Publication Data

Monroe, Judy.
  The Susan B. Anthony women's voting rights trial: a headline court case / Judy
Monroe.
    p. cm. – (Headline court cases)
  Includes bibliographical references and index.
  Summary: Examines the efforts to gain the right for women in the United States to vote,
focusing on the trial of Susan B. Anthony for illegally voting in the presidential election
in 1872.
  ISBN 0-7660-1759-1
  1. Women—Suffrage—United States—History—19th century—Juvenile literature.
  2. Women—Suffrage—New York (State)—History—19th century—Juvenile literature.
  3. Election law—United States—Criminal provisions—History—19th century—Juvenile
literature. 4. Anthony, Susan B. (Susan Brownell), 1820-1906—Trials, litigation, etc.—
Juvenile literature. 5. Trials (Political crimes and offenses)—New York
(State)—History—19th century—Juvenile literature. [1. Women—Suffrage. 2. Anthony,
Susan B. (Susan Brownell), 1820-1906—Trials, litigation, etc. 3. Trials (Political crimes
and offenses)] I. Title. II. Series.
  KF4895.Z9 M63 2002
  324.6'23'0973—dc21

                          2001004528

Printed in the United States of America

10 9 8 7 6 5 4 3 2 1

To Our Readers:
We have done our best to make sure that all Internet addresses in this book were active
and appropriate when we went to press. However, the author and publisher have no control over and assume no liability for the material available on those Internet sites or on
other Web sites they may link to. Any comments or suggestions can be sent by e-mail to
comments@enslow.com or to the address on the back cover.

Illustration Credits: All photos are from the Library of Congress, except for
the following: Enslow Publishers, Inc., p. 94; Lucy Tilden Stewart Collection,
Department of Special Collections, The University Library, University of
Illinois at Chicago, p. 30; National Archives and Record Administration's
Northeast Region, New York City, pp. 54, 61; Special Collections, Vassar
College Libraries, p. 13.

Cover Illustration: Nebraska State Historical Society (digitally enhanced).

Contents

chapter one

TO VOTE OR NOT TO VOTE?

REGISTRATION—On Friday, November 1, 1872, in Rochester, New York, Susan B. Anthony started something bold and daring. She rounded up her three sisters, Guelma, Hannah, and Mary, and her close friend Rhoda DeGarmo, and told them that she had a plan. The four women then walked with Anthony to a local barbershop. This was the place for people to register so they could vote in the presidential election on November 5, 1872.

Three men sat waiting inside. Their job was to sign up *men* to vote. Up until that time, the three had registered only men. Miss Anthony, her sisters, and her friend were there to challenge the male-only voting law in New York State. At that time, state constitutions, and only state constitutions, barred women from voting. (The Fourteenth and Fifteenth Amendments to the U.S. Constitution opened possible ways to change that, but they did not affect women directly in any way.) But, since the Fourteenth Amendment barred *states* from enforcing laws that

A talented organizer and politician, Susan B. Anthony met and influenced thousands of people during her life.

deprived citizens of their rights (including the right to vote), this opened the door for women to vote. In addition, the opening phrase of the Fifteenth Amendment, "The right of citizens of the United States to vote," acknowledged an existing right. Susan B. Anthony hoped to test these interpretations in the courts—to see if the U.S. Constitution, with those two amendments, overrode the New York constitution's bar against women voting.

Because Anthony succeeded in voting, she fell under a totally different law that empowered the federal government to prosecute violations of state voting laws—in this case, a person's knowingly voting without the right to do so. The word "knowingly" became the focus of Susan B. Anthony's eventual trial.

Susan B. Anthony was an American women's rights leader during the 1800s. She worked toward gaining rights for women for most of her life. She believed that *all* United States citizens, not just men, should have equal rights under the U.S. Constitution. Anthony championed many rights for women, but her focus eventually became gaining the right for women to vote.[1] Anthony often told people who asked her why the vote was so important, "The right to vote—[is] the right preservative of all other rights, privileges and immunities [protections]."[2] The right to vote, suffrage, means that all citizens can elect public officials and can adopt or reject proposed ordinances. Without that right, women were being left out of the process that would enable them to elect people who would protect their interests in government.

Early Years

Susan Brownell Anthony was born on February 15, 1820. Her father, Daniel Anthony, had built a house near Adams, Massachusetts. Anthony's father, Daniel, was a member of the Quakers, a Christian group founded in 1650. The Quakers criticized him for marrying Lucy, who was a Baptist. However, she followed Quaker practices after her marriage. As Quakers, the Anthony family was against slavery and committed to pacifism, not fighting in wars. Quakers also treated men and women as equals. Both men and women could speak at most Quaker churches (called "meetings"). In fact, Daniel Anthony's sister was a Quaker preacher.

The Anthony family was close and loving. Susan's parents taught her that every person should be useful in the world. Her mother would tell her, "Go and do all the good you can."[3] Susan's three sisters and her parents supported women's suffrage, the right to vote. Susan's two brothers were active in the Kansas struggle against slavery. (In fact, both of them moved to Kansas.) The quarrel over slavery flared in 1854, when Congress passed the Kansas-Nebraska Act. This law created two federal territories, Kansas and Nebraska, and provided that the people of each territory could decide for themselves whether to permit slavery. But bitter conflicts broke out between supporters and opponents of slavery in Kansas. In fact, the territory became known as "Bleeding Kansas." In the end, Kansas joined the Union as a free state in 1861, but it was a long, bloody struggle.

Daniel Anthony was a farmer, and he ran a small cotton

mill on his land. Lucy Read Anthony kept house for her family. She also took in young women, sometimes as many as eleven at a time, as boarders. These young women helped run the cotton mill. Susan, her sisters, and her mother worked hard every day. They sewed, cleaned, hauled water, prepared meals, and washed dishes. They often worked more than twelve hours a day.

Daniel and Lucy Anthony made sure that their children were educated. At this time, boys went to school, but formal education for girls beyond the primary level was uncommon. All of the Anthony children went to the local school. Even as a young girl, Susan showed an independent spirit. While in school, she asked her male teacher why girls were not shown how to do long division. The teacher said, "A girl needs to know how to read her Bible and count her egg money, nothing more."[4] (Egg money was spending money.) Unsatisfied with this answer, she moved her desk to sit behind the teacher. That way, she could see and hear how he taught long division to the boys.

After a while, Daniel Anthony pulled his children out of school and taught them at home. Later he hired various teachers to continue the children's education at home. Susan B. Anthony stopped using "Brownell" as her middle name when she was a teen, preferring to use simply "B."

At the age of fifteen, Susan B. Anthony and her older sister, Guelma, began teaching. Each earned $1.50 a week, about 25 percent of what male teachers were paid. Women usually were paid a fraction of what men earned for the same jobs.

Because of her father's strong belief in education, Susan B. Anthony continued her own schooling when she was seventeen at a Quaker boarding school. This was an advanced school for girls. That did not last long, though. The country began struggling with a depression, or economic hard times. Daniel Anthony went bankrupt. He lost all his money and was forced to sell his house, store, and factory. Even the household belongings were sold at a public auction. To support herself and help her family, Susan left home and took teaching jobs wherever she could find them.

Better Times

By 1845, Daniel Anthony had received some money from a relative and had purchased a farm near Rochester, New York, close to the Erie Canal. The family's finances started to improve, and Susan B. Anthony was invited to come home. She decided, instead, to keep teaching.

She took a job as head teacher of the female department at Canajoharie Academy in 1846 and stayed for three years. For teaching twenty to twenty-five girls, she received about $100 a year. This was good money at that time, and she spent her earnings as she wished. She lived with relatives in the town.

Anthony began to take pleasure in dressing up a bit. Her parents had always followed a plain style of clothing, as dictated by their religion. Susan B. Anthony and her family had dressed simply, in dark clothing, without any frills. Now Anthony wrote her mother that she had ribbons and flowers on a new hat and that her new dress had four colors.

She also received two marriage proposals. Other men took her on carriage rides and to dances. Men continued to pursue her during the next several decades. However, Susan B. Anthony never married. Her interests and energies lay elsewhere. She later explained, "I never felt I could give up my life of freedom to become a man's housekeeper."[5]

Women had few occupational choices at this time. Many married, had children, and ran their family's household. The work was long and never ending. If they remained single, many lived with and took care of their parents. Susan B. Anthony stayed single by choice. Meanwhile, she looked for ways to make a difference in the world.

Finding Causes

One cause Susan B. Anthony joined was the temperance movement, which sought to prohibit or limit the sale and consumption of alcohol. Public drunkenness was often a problem during this time. In addition, money that husbands spent on alcohol was money that did not help the stay-at-home wives pay the family's bills. Speaking for temperance, Anthony also encouraged women to find legal ways to protect themselves from men who became abusive after drinking too much.

Starting in 1848, she became involved with a local temperance group. On March 2, 1849, she gave her first public speech to some two hundred people. This experience helped start her on the road to transforming the country.

Susan B. Anthony resigned from teaching in the fall of 1851 and moved home with her parents to help run the family farm. In addition, she joined the Rochester, New York, chapter of the Daughters of Temperance and began to organize suppers and fairs to promote the cause. As word of her organizational and speaking talents spread, she traveled to neighboring towns to show other women how to promote temperance. She found, along the way, that she had many supporters.

Antislavery Actions

Susan B. Anthony and her family also challenged the acceptance of slavery in parts of the United States. The Anthony family helped runaway slaves get away from slave states and into freedom in Canada on the Underground Railroad. On Sunday afternoons, their farm became a meeting place for antislavery activists, including Frederick Douglass. Douglass was born a slave in Maryland in 1817 and lived until 1895. He became a famous African-American antislavery and suffrage speaker. Like Douglass, Susan B. Anthony worked for the American Anti-Slavery Society and later became an agent for the society in 1856. She arranged meetings, made speeches, put up posters, and distributed literature. Some

As a young woman, Susan B. Anthony taught school and looked for ways to make a difference in the world.

people fought against her messages in support of temperance and against slavery by making armed threats and throwing things at her.

By 1852, Susan B. Anthony had started linking temperance and women's suffrage in her speeches. At the time, women were considered property. They had no rights in marriage. Their husbands held all the power. Therefore, husbands who abused their wives (perhaps because they drank too much) received no legal consequences. Susan B. Anthony wanted to change this. She attended her first women's rights convention in 1852. She began to urge women to vote for temperance at the ballot boxes. Newspaper editors attacked her for suggesting something so ridiculous. After all, they pointed out, only men could vote.

Promoting Rights

As Susan B. Anthony traveled and broadened her experiences, she began to speak more and more about women's rights and the need for women to be able to vote. She also circulated petitions asking for married women to gain the right to own property.

On December 25, 1854, she began an ambitious plan—to travel to all of New York's fifty-four counties and lecture to people, to sell New Yorkers on the idea of married women having the right to vote and own property. She met her goal during five months of snow and bitter cold. She traveled by train to the larger cities and by sleigh and carriage to the small towns.

Anthony organized and ran the campaign throughout

New York. At each stop, she asked people to sign a petition asking for suffrage and the right of married women to own property. For her lectures, Anthony charged twenty-five cents per person. Still, she often did not earn enough money to pay for her meeting place rentals, transportation, food, and lodging. So she used her own savings.

Many women and some men came to listen to Anthony simply because they never had heard a woman speak in public before. Others came because of her message of women's rights. Even a few newspaper reporters wrote about Anthony's skills as a public speaker. In 1860, New York State lawmakers passed the Married Women's Property Law. Now women in that state had the legal right to own property, conduct business, keep their own wages, and sue.

Susan B. Anthony continued to speak about suffrage as she broadened her travels to include other states. She dealt constantly with poor traveling conditions; dirty, bug-infested lodgings; and bad food. She worked hard and usually traveled alone by train and sometimes horse-drawn coach. It was very unusual for women at that time to travel alone. So Anthony stood out wherever she went.

Along with her suffrage work, Anthony spoke about other causes. One was equal education rights. In 1857, in New York, she said that education should be for all, including women and African Americans. Two years later, she told a New York State Teacher's Convention that educational opportunities needed to exist for all. She believed that all schools and colleges should admit women, ex-slaves, and children of ex-slaves, not just white men.

Anthony also continued holding antislavery campaigns. She conducted one in New York in 1861 called "No Union with Slaveholders. No Compromise." Two years later, Anthony and her close friend Elizabeth Cady Stanton (1815–1902) launched the Women's Loyal National League (WLNL). This organization, the first national women's political organization, supported and petitioned for passage of the Thirteenth Amendment, which outlawed slavery.

The two friends campaigned for equal rights for African Americans and women, including the right to vote. In 1868, Anthony was busy with another cause. She helped form the Working Women's Associations, or unions. (Unions are groups of workers that push for better working conditions and better pay.) At this time, women were not allowed to join men's unions. The women's unions fought for women, especially those in the publishing and garment trades. Anthony and her co-organizers planned that the Working Women's Associations would come to represent all the trades. In 1870, Anthony formed and was the president of the Workingwomen's Central Association. This organization published reports on women's working conditions and provided educational opportunities for working women.

Women's Suffrage

In 1868, Susan B. Anthony made one of her dreams come true—she launched and was the owner and publisher of a women's suffrage newspaper, based in New York City. She named it *The Revolution.* Under this title were the words, "MEN, THEIR RIGHTS AND NOTHING MORE: WOMEN, THEIR RIGHTS

AND NOTHING LESS." The aim of the newspaper was to establish rights for women that white men already had. The articles, most of which were written by Stanton, explained the need for equal rights. The two women also published articles about other topics such as education, women's history, marriage, and business. Susan B. Anthony did most of the fund-raising to pay for the printing and distribution of the newspaper, which went to about three thousand subscribers nationwide.

Starting in 1869, Susan B. Anthony spent some of the winter months each year visiting Washington, D.C. Her purpose was to influence and educate members of Congress about women's suffrage. She did this by presenting petitions, appeals, and witnesses to the House of Representatives and the Senate. Anthony hit especially hard in January every year, when many suffrage leaders came to Congress to testify before committees about why women should get the vote. From 1869 on, Anthony presented to every

Many political cartoons were published during the 1800s and early 1900s that showed the importance of women's right to vote.

Congress a request to have the federal government grant women the right to vote. She spoke to members of Congress each year for the next forty years.

In May 1870, Anthony and Stanton stopped publishing *The Revolution.* Their main financial backer had pulled out, and they now owed $10,000 to printers and other people. Susan B. Anthony took on this debt herself. She vowed to pay back every cent, which she did, six years later.

Susan B. Anthony continued to travel throughout the United States. Whatever extra money she made from her speeches went to pay her creditors. During the summer of 1870, she focused on the people of the Oregon and Washington territories. These territories were not yet states, and she urged the people there to give women the right to vote.

Over the next two decades, Susan B. Anthony would deliver her speech many times throughout the country. For example, for two months in 1871, Anthony lectured in three Midwestern states, including twelve cities in Illinois and sixteen cities in Michigan and Ohio. When she traveled to the Northwest that same year, she racked up two thousand miles and gave more than sixty speeches. Sometimes she spoke two or three times a day. Along with her lecturing, she organized many women's rights organizations across the country. She also gave away free untold numbers of leaflets, brochures, and pamphlets about women's rights and suffrage.

Anthony spoke of the fact that women could gain their own rights, their own money, their own homes and belongings, if they got the right to vote for people who would support those goals. If women got the right to vote, they would have one of the most basic rights that white men already had. They, too, would then be able to vote for issues that were important to them. Anthony reminded women that they would be better represented if they had a voice in making the laws they would live by.

Anthony was often asked why the right to vote was so important for women. She explained, "the fundamental right of citizenship, the right to voice in the government, is a national right."[6] She also liked to quote Senator Charles Sumner (1811–1874), when he addressed the U.S. Senate in 1866 on why former slaves should be allowed to vote: " 'I plead now for the ballot, as the great guarantee; and the only sufficient guarantee [of rights.]' "[7] Winning the right to vote was the basis for women to advance in other ways. For example, Anthony told people that women needed the right to vote to secure a regular source of income for themselves and their families.

Some women, perhaps fearing change, opposed suffrage. But Anthony's frequent lectures, writings, and appearances served to increase public awareness about the issue.

A New Way?

By 1870, Susan B. Anthony was working on a new idea: That women already had the right to vote under the Fourteenth and Fifteenth Amendments. These amendments did not specifically state that only men could vote. This, Anthony believed, meant that anyone could vote in all states.

Susan B. Anthony tested this new theory when she rounded up her three sisters and a female friend and they registered to vote in the 1872 presidential election. On November 5, she voted for Ulysses S. Grant and members of Congress. The law that empowered the federal government to prosecute violations of state voting laws applied to elections for members of Congress. So, it was on the basis of that ballot that Anthony was prosecuted. What followed made national news.

chapter two

SUFFRAGE HISTORY THROUGH 1872

BACKGROUND—In 1820, the year Susan B. Anthony was born, women had very few rights as individuals. Many people argued that women did not need rights because their sole purpose was to give birth, raise children, and run a household. An article in an 1820 Pittsburgh magazine reported that the duties of married women did not include voting or politics. "A woman in politics is like a monkey in a china shop; she can do no good and may do a great deal of harm."[1]

By the time Anthony attempted to vote in 1872, some progress in women's rights had been made. However, the majority of women throughout the United States still could not legally vote.

A Lack of Rights for Women

In the early 1800s, women faced many restrictions. Nowhere in the world did women have the right to vote. In fact, American women during this time had few or no rights. They could not attend college because

Women had few rights in the early to mid-1800s. Many, when they married, toiled long hours at never-ending household chores under primitive conditions such as this.

no college or university would accept female students. Women were not allowed to speak in public. If they did, people called it indecent behavior.

Women could not go into many professions, including law and medicine. Exceptions were nursing and teaching for middle-class women, and unskilled labor such as domestic service or factory work. Even if they worked outside the home, women made much less money than men did.

Women could not serve on a jury and most were not allowed to testify in court. They could not sign contracts, make a will, keep or invest money, run for office, or own or inherit land or other property such as a house.

Married women faced many restrictions. They could not

seek a divorce or get custody of their children if their husband divorced them. Husbands and fathers took any wages women earned. Even the clothes married women wore were not considered their own.

Basically, American women were considered the property of their husbands (if they were married) or their fathers (if they were unmarried). They were totally dependent on men. Once a woman married, she gave up all legal rights and property. Husbands had legal power over their wives and could do what they wanted to their wives, including beating or imprisoning them.

The right to vote was a way for women to gain one of the most important rights that white men already had. And, once women had this right, they could gain other rights as equal citizens. To obtain the right to vote, women would have to:

- Persuade every state to allow women to vote under the rules of their state constitution. Each state, under the U.S. Constitution, can set the rules that qualify people to vote; or

- Convince Congress to pass an amendment to the U.S. Constitution to bar states from denying women the right to vote.

The road to gaining the vote for women began in earnest in 1848.

Women Make News

In early July 1848, a group of five women and two men met in Seneca Falls, New York, for afternoon tea. Their talk turned into a heated discussion about the lack of women's rights. The group decided to hold a public meeting to continue and broaden the discussion. Never before had a public meeting to discuss women's rights been held in the United States.

The group put a small ad in the *Seneca County Courier* newspaper on July 11, 1848. They called their meeting a Woman's Rights Convention and invited anyone interested to attend on July 19 and 20, starting at 10:00 A.M. The location was the Wesleyan Chapel in Seneca Falls.

How should the discussions be held? At first, the women and men could not decide. Then one member of the group, Elizabeth Cady Stanton, drafted a Declaration of Sentiments that listed the oppressions of women. It was similar in format to the rights of revolution listed in the Declaration of Independence.

Over three hundred people attended the convention, many more than the group had thought would attend. Stanton presented the declaration. Sixty-eight women and thirty-two men passed and signed this unique document on July 20, 1848. Stanton next presented eleven resolutions, rights for women, for the convention to pass. All but one, number nine, passed without problem. Number nine asked for the right of women to vote. At this time, no place in the world allowed women to vote. After a great deal of debate over this novel and bold idea, this resolution was also accepted. The women's rights movement was born.

News of the convention and the resulting declaration was reported in the country's newspapers. Based on this historic event, other small groups of women and men began to meet across the United States to continue the discussion of women's rights. Two weeks after the Seneca Falls Convention, a second women's rights convention was held in Rochester, New York.

Susan B. Anthony's parents, Daniel and Lucy Anthony, signed the declaration, as did Mary, their youngest daughter. Susan B. Anthony did not attend. Instead, she was putting her efforts into another cause—temperance. Most states had at least one temperance organization by 1832. One year later, the American Temperance Union was formed.

A Remarkable Friendship

Susan B. Anthony continued her push for temperance and also spoke out against slavery. In May 1851, Elizabeth Cady Stanton and Susan B. Anthony met for the first time. The two women formed a strong friendship right away. Together, they began to speak out against slavery and for temperance.

In September 1852, in Syracuse, New York, Anthony went to her first Woman's Rights Convention. She was elected secretary and read a speech written by her friend Elizabeth Cady Stanton. Anthony's clear voice traveled throughout the meeting hall. She urged women not to pay taxes if they owned property and not to attend churches where they did not have equal opportunity to participate on the same level as the men. Other women also spoke about women's rights during the convention.

Local newspapers did not take seriously the idea of women voting. Anthony, however, started to become more outspoken about the fact that women needed the right to

Elizabeth Cady Stanton (seated) and Susan B. Anthony made a strong team working for women's rights; Stanton was a powerful writer and Anthony was an electrifying speaker.

vote. She traveled from town to town, carrying the messages of temperance and suffrage. After her speeches, articles in the local newspapers often attacked her messages. At this time, women seldom spoke out in public about issues.

Susan B. Anthony also worked with Elizabeth Cady Stanton and other women to ask New York lawmakers to pass an amendment granting married women the right to own property. Stanton, with Anthony's help, wrote and delivered a speech to a joint session of New York lawmakers in March 1860. Thanks to the work of Anthony, Stanton, and others, the amendment was passed. Married women in New York now had new rights: they could own property, earn and keep their own wages, enter into contracts, and sue. Women in New York were no longer considered the property of their husbands. They could divorce their husbands and get custody of their children if they divorced. This law was the first of its kind for American women.

Stanton and Anthony made a good team spreading the word about women's rights and suffrage. Anthony was a talented speaker, organizer, politician, and editor. She planned meetings and helped guide people in their work for women's rights. Stanton was a powerful writer. Her words helped people understand the need for women's rights.

Stanton later explained their working relationship as, "I forged the thunderbolts and she [Anthony] fired them."[2] Henry B. Stanton, Elizabeth Cady Stanton's husband, once said to her, "You stir up Susan & she stirs the world."[3] The two also worked with many other women suffragists.

Civil War Years

After Abraham Lincoln was elected president in 1860, the issue of slavery became more heated between the states. The Civil War broke out in April 1861. This war ran until 1865 and pitted the Union (the North) and the Confederacy (the South) against each other. Anthony had arranged for the annual National Woman's Rights Convention to be held in May in New York. However, she dropped the idea, as the war consumed most people's energies and time.

Anthony, Stanton, and other suffrage workers put aside their demands for the vote during the Civil War and concentrated instead on abolishing slavery. Anthony, Stanton, Lucy Stone (another women's suffragist), and others created the Women's Loyal National League in 1863. They put together a plan to collect signatures on petitions to ask for the freedom of all slaves in America. They gathered four hundred thousand signatures by the summer of 1864, which ranked as the largest petition campaign in American history up to that time.[4]

Both Northern and Southern women raised money for the war and gave food and clothing to soldiers. Thousands of women became nurses. Others ran the family farms while their husbands and older sons were at war.

The Fourteenth and Fifteenth Amendments

After the Civil War ended, Susan B. Anthony and Elizabeth Cady Stanton collected signatures on petitions asking Congress to include women's suffrage in the Fourteenth Amendment. By January 1866, these petitions began to reach Congress. That same year, Anthony and Stanton formed the American Equal Rights Association. This organization for white and African-American women and men was dedicated to the goal of suffrage for all. Anthony told supporters that the organization did this to "broaden our woman's rights platform and make it in name what it has ever been in spirit, a human rights platform."[5] Anthony meant that she wanted all citizens in the United States to have equal rights—including the right to vote, the right to be represented in government, and the ability to influence the passage of laws.

The next year seemed to offer some hope on suffrage for New York women. A state constitutional convention in June planned to look at changing the state's constitution.

Anthony and Stanton formed a suffrage campaign in New York. They traveled through all the counties, asking women to sign petitions for suffrage. They signed up over twenty-eight thousand women who said that they wanted to vote.[6] However, New York's male voters successfully opposed women's right to vote.

Meanwhile, Lucy Stone and her husband, Henry Blackwell, launched a suffrage campaign in Kansas. The campaign was not going well there, either. Stone wrote her friends to come and help, and Anthony and Stanton responded, arriving in Kansas in September 1867. They pushed across the state, speaking along the way about suffrage. Their hard work proved fruitless, however, when the vote for women did not pass in Kansas.

Anthony and Stanton opposed the Fourteenth

Many newspapers of the day ridiculed the fight for women's suffrage. Here, a cartoon from 1875 shows Susan B. Anthony, Elizabeth Cady Stanton, and their colleague Anna Dickinson wearing men's shorts and trousers.

Amendment in its current form, because it did nothing to grant women the right to vote. Even in their disappointment, Anthony saw something positive for women. She pointed out to supporters that it was the first time women's suffrage was being debated in Congress. They discussed their opposition to the amendment in *The Revolution,* the newspaper Anthony had started in New York. From the start, *The Revolution* received generally favorable reviews for its style and range of topics, including women's suffrage.

Anthony handled ads and subscriptions and paid the printer and office rent. Stanton and Parker Pillsbury (1809–1898), a man who supported women's suffrage and opposed slavery, did most of the writing and editing. Women from around the United States sent information about women's achievements to *The Revolution,* which the newspaper then published.

In *The Revolution,* Anthony and Stanton also asked that women oppose the Fifteenth Amendment, which would give African-American men the right to vote. The two women asked that this amendment be changed to include votes for all citizens, regardless of race or gender. The Fifteenth Amendment, containing no mention of women, passed the House and Senate in 1870 and was then sent to the states for voting. Three fourths of the states needed to pass this amendment before it would become law.

Anthony's and Stanton's protest over the Fifteenth Amendment clashed with the beliefs of other women suffragists and resulted in the development of two competing suffrage groups.

Two Suffrage Groups Form

Anthony, Stanton, Martha Wright, and others founded the National Woman Suffrage Association (NWSA) in May 1869. Stanton was president of the New York–based NWSA. No man could hold office in the organization. Anthony's weekly newspaper, *The Revolution,* until its end in 1870, carried news about the NWSA.

In November 1869, Lucy Stone, Julia Ward Howe, and other women formed the American Woman Suffrage Association (AWSA), centered in Boston, Massachusetts. Men could join, and the AWSA's first president was Reverend Henry Ward Beecher. The AWSA launched its weekly newspaper, *The Woman's Journal,* on January 8, 1870.

Although both organizations sought political equality for women, the NWSA was more outspoken on a broader range of issues than the AWSA. For example, the NWSA wanted all

discrimination against women stopped. Members demanded divorce law reform, an eight-hour workday, equal pay, and access to higher education. In contrast, the AWSA focused solely on gaining the right for women to vote.

Lucy Stone, another prominent suffragist, helped to found the Women's Loyal National League in 1863 and the American Woman Suffrage Association in 1869.

The two groups also differed in their approach to gaining suffrage. The NWSA pressed for a federal (national) women's suffrage law and fought for a Constitutional amendment for women's suffrage. In contrast, the AWSA opted for gradual adoption of women's suffrage on a state-by-state basis.

Some Victories

Suffragists counted two victories in 1870. Both were in the newly settled frontier of the West. In 1869, women were given the right to vote in the territory of Wyoming. When Wyoming was admitted into the Union in 1890, it kept this right for its women. Utah, too, gave women the right to vote in 1870. That right was retained when it became a state in 1896. However, suffragists still had a long road ahead of them.

chapter three

THE ROAD TO COURT

BOLD EFFORTS—By the late 1860s, Susan B. Anthony began to look for new ways to push for women's suffrage. One way was to see what women were attempting in England, as they, too, sought the vote. Anthony also began to hear about people who were reexamining the U.S. Constitution and its amendments. There, some argued, lay the answer—that women already had suffrage. Susan B. Anthony listened, read, debated, and in the end, decided to vote in the 1872 presidential election, based on her conviction that women already had the constitutional right to vote.

English Women Also Fight for Suffrage

In 1867 and 1868, women in England had tried to prove that the legal rights of women allowed female property owners the right to vote for representatives in Parliament. Similar to the American Congress, the Parliament of Great Britain is the lawmaking body of that nation.

However, when women who owned property in Manchester, England, asked for a ruling from the Parliament, they were disappointed. The court said "every woman is personally incapable" of making legal decisions such as voting.[1]

Victoria Woodhull Speaks to Congress

Victoria Woodhull (1838–1927) owned a brokerage firm in the financial district of New York City. This was very unusual for a woman at that time. She was also a strong supporter of women's rights and the first woman to run for president (in 1872). In January 1871, Victoria Woodhull was allowed to speak before the judiciary committee of the U.S. House of Representatives. She argued that women had the right to vote under the Fourteenth and Fifteenth Amendments to the Constitution. Woodhull finished by asking for Congress to allow voting rights and property ownership for women under the two amendments.

Woodhull's speech to Congress built on legal interpretations of the Constitution and the two amendments. She argued, "A race of people comprises all the people, male and female. The right to vote cannot be denied on account of race."[2]

Susan B. Anthony congratulated Woodhull after her presentation. She then brought Woodhull to the annual NWSA convention that was to be held that same day. Woodhull repeated her speech to the assembled women.

One month later, Representative John A. Bingham of Ohio, chair of the judiciary committee, issued a committee report. The judiciary committee denied Woodhull's request for a congressional act. The committee disagreed with

Woodhull, saying that the Fourteenth and Fifteenth Amendments did not give women the right to vote.

Voting Attempts By Women

Meanwhile, some women took the law into their own hands and tried to vote in their own states. Susan B. Anthony reported these cases in *The Revolution.* In Vineland, New Jersey, some women tried to vote in 1868 but were unsuccessful. A year later, after reading about voting rights in Wyoming in 1869, Mary Olney Brown and her sister, Charlotte Olney French, voted in the Washington Territory. Another woman, Marilla Ricker, registered and voted in New Hampshire a year later. In 1871 and 1872, over one hundred fifty women tried to vote in ten states. The registrars blocked most women from voting, although some succeeded.[3]

For example, in 1871, two women in Detroit, Michigan, one woman in Illinois, one woman in Santa Cruz, California, and another woman in Philadelphia, Pennsylvania, all registered and tried to vote. Only one vote out of the five, that of Nannette Gardener of Detroit, was accepted. That same year, seventy-two women tried unsuccessfully to register and vote in the District of Columbia. When their votes were refused, they brought their case to the Supreme Court of the District of Columbia.

During this time, another case had made its way before members of the U.S. Supreme Court. Myra Bradwell was one of America's first female lawyers. The Illinois Supreme Court had turned her away from admission into the Illinois bar because Bradwell was a married woman. Without admission to the state bar, Bradwell could not practice law in Illinois. The Supreme Court heard Bradwell's case and ruled that the state of Illinois had not violated the federal Constitution. This meant Bradwell could not practice law in the state of Illinois. It was yet another setback for women's rights.

Susan B. Anthony was not put off by these setbacks. She and Elizabeth Cady Stanton urged women throughout the country to vote. They called their idea the "New Departure." Meanwhile, Anthony developed her own plan to vote in the upcoming presidential election in November 1872.

Preparations

Susan B. Anthony lived with her family at 7 Madison Street in Rochester, New York, for the thirty days' residency required of voters in the state of New York. Early on the morning of November 1, 1872, Anthony opened the morning newspaper and read,

> Now register! To-day and to-morrow are the only remaining opportunities. If you were not permitted to vote, you would fight for the right, undergo all privations for it, face death for it. You have it now at the cost of five minutes' time to be spent in seeking your place of registration, and having your name entered. . . . Register now![4]

Nothing in the notice indicated that voter registration was strictly for men.

Anthony gathered her legal papers and rounded up her three sisters, Guelma, Hannah, and Mary, and her friend Rhoda DeGarmo. Around 9:00 A.M., the five women walked

Some women tried to force the issue of voting. These three women are casting votes, but, like Susan B. Anthony, had no legal grounds to do so.

into a local barbershop that had been turned into a voting place. Eleven other women joined Anthony's group to register to vote in the presidential election on November 5, 1872.

Three men sat inside. Up until then, only men had registered to vote. Anthony demanded that they be allowed to register. The three men refused, citing the New York constitution. Anthony then pulled out various legal documents to show the men. One of the men at the barbershop, Beverly W. Jones, recalled what happened next.

> She said she was a citizen of the U.S. and demanded her
> right to be registered. I made the remark that I didn't think
> we could register her name. She asked me upon what
> grounds. I told her that the constitution of the State of New
> York only gave the right of franchise [voting] to male citi-
> zens. She asked me if I was acquainted with the 14th
> Amendment to the U.S. Constitution. I told her I was. She
> wanted to know if under that she was a citizen and had a
> right to vote. At this time, Mr. Warner [another of the men at
> the barbershop] said, young man, how are you going to get
> around that. I think you will have to register their names—
> or something to that effect.[5]

Anthony and Jones talked a little more. Unsure how to
handle this situation, the men turned to John Van Voorhis, a
lawyer, for advice. Van Voorhis, a supporter of women's suffrage, recommended that the women be registered. Jones
said that one of the other men spoke up then. "He was in
favor of registering their names & I concurred."[6]

Finally, Jones and Edwin F. Marsh agreed to register
Anthony, her sisters, her friend, and the other women.

The local evening papers reported Anthony's actions and
said the men should be arrested for registering the women.
Inspired by Anthony's bold act, about fifty other Rochester
women registered to vote during the week of voter registration. News of Anthony's daring feat did not hit the national
newspapers until later.

Waiting to Vote

Anthony and the other registered women had a few days
until Election Day. Meanwhile, one Rochester daily
newspaper editor researched the possible result of Anthony's

actions. He printed a warning in his newspaper that anyone who voted without having a legal right to do so could be found guilty of a crime. If convicted by the federal court, that person could be fined up to $500, put in prison for up to three years, or both.

Anthony returned to the barbershop to talk to the men and asked them to hold firm. Also, she promised to cover any legal costs that resulted from their actions. The federal government could arrest not only Anthony, but the men. The men could be charged with illegally registering the women to vote.

Anthony had gone to see a lawyer to get advice before she voted. That Saturday, she walked to the offices of various lawyers. None would consider her case. Finally, Henry R. Selden, a former judge of the court of appeals, listened to her. Selden was a lawyer of excellent reputation in Rochester. He heard Anthony's information and asked that she leave the legal arguments proposed by others with him for review.

Selden met with Anthony the next Monday morning. He told her that the registered women had a good case for the constitutional right to vote. He added, "I will protect you in that right to the best of my ability."[7] Anthony informed the women of this legal advice and all promised to show up the next morning to vote.

Voting Day

On Tuesday, Election Day, November 5, 1872, Anthony walked into the barbershop to vote. It was 7:00 A.M. She arrived early to reduce the possibility of creating a public spectacle. She cast her vote for Ulysses S. Grant and two congressmen. Beverly Jones deposited Anthony's ballots in the proper boxes. While voting, Anthony was challenged by Sylvester Lewis, a registrar. Jones showed Lewis that Anthony was officially registered and sworn in to vote. Anthony met with no other obstacles while she voted.

Anthony was in high spirits over her daring feat. She immediately wrote to Stanton, "Well I have been & gone & done it!! Positively voted the Republican ticket—straight—this AM at 7 o'clock and swore my vote in at that—fifteen other women followed suit in this ward. . . . So we are in for fine agitation in Rochester."[8]

Although Anthony had urged many women to vote on Election Day, the female turnout was low. A few women tried to vote in Michigan, Missouri, Ohio, and Connecticut. The Rochester, New York, registrars who had allowed fifty women to register would not allow them to vote. Stanton did not try to register or vote.

As always, Anthony supported fellow suffragists. In a letter to Sarah Huntington, who had tried to vote, she wrote, "I rejoice to see your attempt to vote in old Connecticut.... To vote is our wish."[9]

Anthony's brave move was telegraphed across the country, and many newspapers carried the story. By the age of fifty-two, Susan B. Anthony had obtained celebrity status. Her voting attempt made big news. The responses in newspapers were generally complimentary. For example, an article in *The New York Times* said, "The act of Susan B.

As this cartoon shows, some people feared that if women got the right to vote, they would no longer want to stay at home.

Anthony should have a place in history."[10] Some newspaper editors, though, felt that her ballot for Grant showed that women were unfit for voting. (This indicates that the editors disagreed with the majority of U.S. voters—since Grant won the election.)

Anthony Is Arrested

Ulysses S. Grant won the election, and Susan B. Anthony's bold actions slipped out of the headlines. On November 14, a warrant for her arrest was written up. It said that she had voted on November 5, 1872, but "without having a lawful right to vote. . . ."[11]

Two weeks after that, on November 28, Thanksgiving Day, U.S. Marshal E. J. Keeney came to 7 Madison Street. (A United States marshal has the legal right to enforce federal law anywhere in the country.) Keeney was there to arrest Susan B. Anthony for illegally voting. The marshal said there was no hurry for Anthony to appear before the U.S. commissioner and she could go alone. In fact, the commissioner would be pleased whenever she came in, he said.

Anthony was not impressed by his politeness and asked, "Is this your usual method of serving a warrant?"[12] The warrant stated:

> Without having a lawful right to vote in said election district the said Susan B. Anthony, being then and there a person of the female sex, as she, the said Susan B. Anthony, then and there well known contrary to the statute of the United States of America in such cases made and provided, and against the peace of the United States . . . did knowingly . . . and unlawfully vote.[13]

Anthony had violated Section 19 of an act of Congress. This act, or law, said anyone who voted illegally was guilty of a crime. If charged with the crime by a federal judge and found guilty, she could be fined up to $500 or put into jail for up to three years.

Anthony refused any special treatment by the marshal except to be allowed to go upstairs to change her dress. She came downstairs and held out her wrists to be handcuffed, but Keeney had no handcuffs. The two then went downtown by a horse-drawn streetcar. Anthony hoped to gain publicity as a result of her arrest. She loudly told the streetcar conductor to ask the marshal to pay her five-cent fare, since the federal government had arrested her. Of course, people on the streetcar heard her.

Charged With a Crime

When Anthony arrived at the office of U.S. Commissioner William C. Storrs, she saw that the male registrars and the other women who had voted in her area had also been arrested. They all waited until early evening, when they were told that Richard Crowley, the district attorney for the government, had not arrived yet, so they could go home for the day. They were told to return in the morning. (The district attorney, or prosecutor, is a government official who is authorized to accuse and bring to trial someone who is believed to have committed a crime.)

The next morning, Friday, Anthony and the other women voters returned, along with crowds of other women who came to hear her speak. Later, during her examination,

Crowley asked if she had voted to test the question of her constitutional right to vote. Anthony replied, "Yes, sir; I had been resolved for three years to vote at the first election when I had been at home for thirty days before."[14]

A date for her preliminary hearing was set. (A preliminary hearing is called for when someone is accused of a felony, a serious crime generally punishable by imprisonment or sometimes death.)

Anthony said she had some presentations scheduled through December 10 and could not make the assigned date. Crowley scolded her, saying that she was supposed to be in custody until that time and could not leave the area. Anthony ignored him and continued her speaking tours.

The second hearing for Anthony, the other women, and the registrars was held on December 23. All pleaded not guilty. Their case was sent to a grand jury, a group of people who decide if there is enough evidence of a crime to warrant a trial. The women were ordered to attend a trial, and each was released on $500 bail. (Bail is an amount of money paid by people who have been arrested so that they can be temporarily released from custody. They must also promise to appear in court at a later date.) Everyone but Anthony paid the bail. Anthony's bail was then increased to $1,000.

On January 10, 1873, Anthony's lawyer applied for a writ of habeas corpus. This is a legal document that protects people against illegal imprisonment. In this case, Anthony and her lawyer were challenging the reason for her imprisonment. She argued that she had not committed a crime but had instead exercised a right—the right to vote. Anthony took this path for a reason. If she challenged this law but lost in court, she could take her case to the U.S. Supreme Court. This would bring suffrage to national action. Her lawyer asked the judge to "send the writ by mail" so that it "will be presented in Miss Anthony's case."[15] While waiting for a reply to the writ, Anthony was released until her next trial date.

Anthony seemed surprised at what had happened. On January 1, 1873, she wrote to a friend, "I never dreamed of the U.S. officers prosecuting me for voting—thought only if I was refused—I should bring action against inspectors [registrars]."[16]

About a month later, on January 21, 1873, Anthony and her lawyer stood before a U.S. district judge in Albany. He listened to the reasons for a writ of habeas corpus, then denied the writ.

Anthony's lawyer told her to take his legal advice and that he would pay her bail. Anthony said no. However, he wrote a check for her bail. Anthony was free to go.

The story goes that as they were walking out of the courthouse, the two met John Van Voorhis, an attorney who was working with Selden on her case. They told him what had happened. Then Anthony found out what she had lost: Van Voorhis told them that by paying bail, she had lost her chance to go to the Supreme Court by writ of habeas corpus. Anthony rushed back into the courtroom to try to withdraw the bail, but she was too late. The bail had been legally recorded and could not be withdrawn.

Coming back out of the courtroom, Anthony asked

Selden if he knew the results of his actions. He said "Yes, but I could not see a lady I respected put in jail."[17]

Pretrial Events

At the federal grand jury hearing in Albany, New York, on January 22, 1873, twenty male grand jurors indicted Anthony. An indictment is a formal, written accusation of a crime. It also names the person who probably committed the crime. Her trial was set for May 13, 1873, in Rochester, New York.

Anthony did not waste time thinking about her coming trial. Instead, she spoke to potential jurors about women's suffrage. She traveled throughout Monroe County, where she would be tried, lecturing. Her speech was called, "Is It a Crime for a Citizen of the U.S. to Vote?" She spoke in twenty-nine towns and villages.

On March 4, Anthony voted in a local election. Two others joined her. She also printed and distributed copies of her lawyer's arguments for women's right to vote to editors and congressmen in New York and Washington, D.C. Anthony even squeezed in lectures in Ohio, Indiana, and Illinois to promote suffrage.

Wherever Anthony spoke, the press was there. Already famous, she was made even more of a celebrity by her arrest and upcoming trial. Some newspapers supported suffrage and her actions. Others ridiculed suffrage and Susan B. Anthony.

Because of her extensive speaking, the prosecutor said that no neutral jurors were left in Monroe County. In mid-May, he asked the judge if her trial could be moved to a new location, the U.S. Circuit Court at Canandaigua, Ontario County, New York. This request was granted.

Anthony had little time to canvass Ontario County. In less than a month, though, she spoke in over twenty towns. A friend and fellow suffragist, Matilda Joslyn Gage, helped out by speaking in sixteen towns. Gage called her speech, "The United States on Trial, Not Susan B. Anthony."

The Judge and Jury

Before Anthony's trial officially began, Judge Ward Hunt was appointed to the case. He was a state supreme court justice serving in circuit court. He was also staunchly opposed to the idea of women's suffrage. The case had been postponed to ensure it came before him.

During a trial, a judge should not take sides. The duties of a judge include:

- listening to evidence;

- making certain the accused's constitutional rights are protected;

- making certain proper legal procedures are followed; and

- listening when the lawyers argue over evidence, then deciding, based on rules of evidence, if the evidence should be admitted into the trial. Evidence is any statement or object that can be presented in a court case as a proof of fact.

The judge and the lawyers for both sides selected the people who would be on the jury. No legal record is recorded about the selection process. However, at this time, New York jurors had to be male, residents of New York, between the ages of twenty-one and sixty, and owners of property.

Jurors must be impartial, or not biased against the defendant. The duties of a jury include:

- evaluating the evidence presented at the trial;

- deciding if the accused is guilty beyond a reasonable doubt (reasonable doubt is the highest level of certainty a juror must have in the court system to find a defendant guilty of a crime);

- reaching a unanimous decision after hearing all the evidence at the trial; and

- announcing the verdict, or decision, to the accused and judge.

Although the courtroom was always crowded during Anthony's trial, people were quiet. Judge Hunt maintained a serious tone throughout the trial. The publicity surrounding the trial, and Anthony's national status as a women's activist, stirred people's excitement. This was the emotionally charged setting under which Susan B. Anthony's trial officially began.

chapter four

THE TRIAL

ROCHESTER, N.Y.—The trial of Susan B. Anthony began on June 17, 1873, at 2:30 P.M. The courthouse held to tradition by ringing its tower bell to announce the opening of court sessions. For her role as the ringleader, Anthony was the only Rochester woman voter who was put on trial. The federal government decided not to try the other Rochester women who had voted.

In a federal criminal case, the government accuses and prosecutes, or brings to trial, a suspected criminal. The United States government charged Susan B. Anthony with voting illegally in a national election. The facts of the case, called the *United States of America* v. *Susan B. Anthony*, would fill dozens of handwritten pages of court documents.

The Trial Process

To present the facts during a trial, each side calls witnesses. These people come to the witness stand and swear to give truthful testimony or information. Each side can also present evidence. Evidence is any physical item relevant to the trial. This can include documents or letters.

During a criminal trial, both sides present their witnesses and evidence to the jury—first the prosecution (the government), then the defense. During this process, witnesses are asked questions. Each side calls its own witnesses and questions them on direct examination. This means that they may ask only direct questions, not open-ended questions that do not suggest a specific answer. For example, "Where were you at 7:00 A.M. on November 5, 1873?" is a direct question.

The prosecuting attorney presents his witnesses and evidence first. The prosecutor tries to convince the jury that the defendant is guilty of the charge. The defense then questions the prosecution's witnesses to try to show that the witnesses are not believable, are incorrect, or are prejudiced against the defendant. This process is called cross-examination.

Here is what the courtroom looked like during Anthony's trial:

Judge Ward Hunt	
Trial Clerk	**Witness Stand**
Defendant Susan B. Anthony	**12 Male Jurors**
Defense Lawyers • Henry R. Selden • John Van Voorhis	**Federal Government's Prosecuting Lawyer** • Richard Crowley, U.S. District Attorney

On the morning of the trial, the court crier announced Judge Ward Hunt, and everyone in the courtroom stood as the judge entered the room. He ordered the trial to begin. The courtroom on the second floor was packed with friends of Anthony's, members of the general public, and reporters. Included in the mix were several prosuffrage U.S. senators and one ex-president, Millard Fillmore.

The Prosecution's Opening Statement

Susan B. Anthony's trial officially began with an opening statement by the prosecution. Opening statements summarize the strong points of each side's case and tell what each side intends to prove during the trial. However, nothing the lawyers say during the opening can be used as evidence.

The crowded courtroom heard the prosecutor, U.S. District Attorney Richard Crowley, say that Susan B. Anthony had voted in a federal election on November 5, 1872. He said that when she voted,

> At that time she was a woman. I suppose there will be no question about that. The question in this case, if there be a question of fact about it at all, will, in my judgment, be rather a question of law than one of fact. I suppose . . . it will be for you [the jury] to decide under the charge of his honor, the Judge, whether or not the defendant committed the offence of voting. . . .[1]

The Prosecution's Witnesses

The federal government called only two witnesses to testify. The first witness established the basic facts of the case:

Anthony was female, she was registered to vote, and she did vote in a federal election. The second witness said that Anthony had developed a plan to vote long before the election actually arrived.

Beverly W. Jones

The prosecution's first witness was Beverly W. Jones, one of the men who had allowed Anthony to register to vote. Under questioning by Crowley, Jones first provided information about himself and about his job as a registrar. Then Crowley asked if Jones had seen Anthony vote. Jones replied that he had.

Crowley continued, "Did you receive the tickets [voting ballots] from Miss Anthony?"[2] Jones said he had received them and put them in the correct voting boxes.

It is important to remember that despite the fact that Susan B. Anthony asserted her right to vote under the Fourteenth Amendment to the U.S. Constitution, she still broke the laws of New York—which strictly forbade women to vote.

Selden now cross-examined Jones. (Cross-examination is the questioning of a witness in a trial by the opposing side's attorney.) He asked, "When the registry was being made did Miss Anthony appear before the Board of Registry and claim to be registered as a voter?"[3] Yes, said Jones, adding that objections were raised as to her right to vote. That was, he said, because the "Constitution of the State of New York did not allow women to vote."[4]

Selden asked, "What was the defect in her right to vote

And thereupon *Richard Crowley* Esq., the Attorney of the United States for the said District, prayed the process of the said *District* Court for the arrest of the said *Susan B. Anthony* and it was granted ; and on the *27th* day of *January* in the year of our Lord one thousand eight hundred and seventy- *nine* of the *January* term of *said Court* at the *City* of *Albany* came the Marshal of the United States for the Northern District of New York, and brought into the said *District* Court the body of the said *Susan B. Anthony* upon the said process : and the said

Susan B. Anthony

being duly arraigned upon the said Indictment *, and being* called upon to plead thereto, pleaded that she was *not* guilty of the offenses charged therein, in manner and form as the same are therein set forth, and of this she put *herself* upon the country, and said United States of America did the like. *at the May term of said District Court, held at the city of Rochester on the 22 day of May,* And, *thereupon* the said *Richard Crowley* the Attorney of the United States, for the Northern District of New York, moved that the said Indictment and the issue joined thereon be transmitted to the *Circuit* Court of the United States for the said Northern District of New York for disposal therein, and the said motion was granted.

Wherefore let a jury be summoned, empanelled and sworn to try the said issue at the *June* term of said Court in the year of our Lord one thousand eight hundred and seventy- *three* at the *Village* of *Canandaigua* in the said District. And now on *the 17th & 18th* day of *June* of the term of *June* one thousand eight hundred and seventy- *three* aforesaid come as well the Attorney of the United States for the said District as the said *Susan B. Anthony* and come also the jurors aforesaid ;

and the said jurors to speak the truth of the matters within contained being chosen, tried and sworn upon their oaths say, that the said *Susan B. Anthony* is guilty *on June 19th* of the offenses charged in the said Indictment in manner and form as the same are therein set forth. And, *there* upon the said *Susan B. Anthony* being present in open Court, and having heard the said verdict is inquired of by the Court if she has anything to say why the judgment of the law should not be pronounced upon her according to the said verdict : and no sufficient answer being given, His Honor the Judge of the said Court, in the presence of the said *Susan B. Anthony* does here adjudge and sentence that the said *Susan B. Anthony* for the said offenses of which she stands convicted as aforesaid be imprisoned in the at hard labor for the term of years and months and pay a fine of *one hundred dollars and the costs of this prosecution*

Charles Mason
Clerk.

This shows some of the court proceedings from Anthony's trial.

as a citizen?"[5] Jones explained, "She was not a male citizen."[6] Jones added that the men discussed whether they should allow Anthony to register to vote. Finally, two registrars, Beverly W. Jones and Edwin T. Marsh, decided she was entitled to register. The third man, William B. Hall, disagreed with the other two. The majority won, and Anthony and the other women were registered.

Crowley reexamined Jones. (In redirect examination, the attorney who originally called a witness has the opportunity to question a witness after he or she has been cross-examined.) His questions and Jones's answers showed that Anthony had claimed the right to vote under the Fourteenth Amendment to the Constitution of the United States. Finally, Crowley verified that Anthony was registered on the poll list (a list of people who registered to vote), and that she had voted on November 5, 1872.

John E. Pound

John E. Pound was the assistant U.S. district attorney for the northern district of New York, where Anthony had voted. After being sworn in as a witness, he told the jury that he had attended the pretrial hearings of Anthony in Rochester. He confirmed that Anthony had been registered and had voted. Crowley then asked if the advice Henry R. Selden had given to Anthony had made a difference in her decision to vote.

Pound remembered that Anthony said, "I should have made the same endeavor to vote that I did had I not consulted Judge Selden. . . . I was not influenced by his advice in the matter at all; have been resolved to vote, the first time I was at home 30 days, for a number of years."[7]

John Van Voorhis, one of Anthony's attorneys, asked Pound whether Anthony had expressed doubts about her right to vote. Pound answered that Anthony "had no doubt" about her right.[8]

The U.S. government did not present any more witnesses. It was now the defense's turn. Henry Selden got up, strode to the front of the courtroom, and spoke for the defendant, Susan B. Anthony.

The Defense's Opening Statement

The defense lawyers were head attorney Henry R. Selden and John Van Voorhis. The defense tried to prove that Anthony was not guilty of knowingly breaking the law. (After all, she truly believed she had the right to vote according to the U.S. Constitution, which takes precedent over New York's laws.) In his opening statement, Selden told the jury:

> I claim and shall endeavor to establish before you that when she offered to have her name registered as a voter . . . she was as much entitled to vote as any man that voted at that election, according to the Constitution and laws of the Government under which she lives. If I maintain that . . . as a matter of course she has committed no offence, and is entitled to be discharged at your hands.
>
> But, beyond that, whether she was a legal voter or not, whether she was entitled to vote or not, if she sincerely believed that she had a right to vote, and offered her ballot in good faith, under that belief, whether right or wrong, by the laws of this country she is guilty of no crime . . . the only

question which, in my judgment, can come before you to be passed upon by you as a question of fact is whether or not she did vote in good faith, believing she had a right to vote. . . . If she was mistaken in that judgment . . . that is not a reason for committing her to a felon's cell [jail].[9]

The defense was telling the jurors that because Susan B. Anthony truly believed she had the legal right to vote (under the Fourteenth and Fifteenth Amendments), she had voted in good faith and therefore had not broken the law.

The Defense's Witnesses

During the remainder of the trial, Selden continued to bolster the claims that Anthony had not committed a crime. The defense built its strategy on three points:

1. Susan B. Anthony truly believed she was legally entitled to vote under the Fourteenth and Fifteenth Amendments of the U.S. Constitution.

2. Even if she were not entitled to vote in New York, she had voted in good faith, believing that it was her right.

3. Because she had voted in good faith, and with this belief, she had not committed a crime.

Selden asked that Anthony be called to the witness stand to testify "on the question of the intention or belief under which she voted."[10] The prosecution protested this request, and Judge Hunt ruled that Susan B. Anthony was incompetent to be a witness. Judge Hunt never allowed Anthony to testify during her own trial.

This drawing shows women at the polls in Cheyenne, Wyoming Territory, in 1888. Wyoming joined the Union in 1890 and became the first state to grant women the right to vote.

Judge Hunt did allow Selden to be a witness for his client. He spoke for three hours and was Anthony's only witness. He pointed out that the only reason Anthony's vote was supposedly illegal was because she was a woman. He testified:

> If the same act had been done by her brother under the same circumstances, the act would have been not only innocent, but honorable and laudable [praiseworthy]; but having been done by a woman it is said to be a crime. . . . I believe this is the first instance in which a woman has been arraigned in a criminal case, merely on account of her sex. . . . Women have the same interest that men have in the establishment and maintenance of good government . . . [they] should be allowed equally with men, to express their preference in the choice of law-makers and rulers. But however that may be, no greater *absurdity,* to use no harsher term, could be presented, than that of rewarding men and punishing women, for the same act. . . .[11]

Selden then claimed that Anthony had voted in good faith. She believed that the Fourteenth and Fifteenth Amendments to the U.S. Constitution gave her the right to vote. She was now being tried as a criminal because she had taken the only step open to her in order to bring this constitutional issue to the courts. Next, Selden discussed the legal interpretations of the two amendments and gave examples of legal cases to support his claims.

At the end of the testimony, Judge Hunt ruled that Anthony's case would continue the next day. Anthony was pleased with her attorney's testimony on her behalf. She wrote in her diary that evening that Selden's speech was "a masterly statement of the [suffrage] cause."[12]

Crowley delivered his two-hour summation (closing

argument) for the prosecution the next day. He said that it did not matter what Anthony's intentions had been when she voted. The fact remained that by voting, Susan B. Anthony had broken the law in New York, and in doing so, was also guilty of committing a federal crime.

The Verdict

Immediately after Crowley finished, Judge Hunt reached in his pocket and brought out a paper. He had prepared in advance his verdict on Anthony's case. He read out loud to the jury:

> The question, gentlemen of the jury . . . is wholly a question or questions of law [and] under the 14th Amendment, which Miss Anthony claims protects her, she was not protected in a right to vote. And I have decided also that her belief and the advice which she took [from her lawyer] does not protect her in the act which she committed. If I am right in this, the result must be a verdict on your [the jury's] part of guilty, and I therefore direct that you [the jury] find a verdict of guilty.[13]

Judge Hunt was asking that the jurors find Susan B. Anthony guilty based on the fact that she had voted, and women were not legally entitled to vote in New York State. The Fourteenth Amendment to the Constitution, according to Judge Hunt, did nothing to protect Anthony. She had no legal right to vote, but she did so anyway. Thus she broke the law. It did not matter what she had been told or what she believed to be true.

As Judge Hunt finished, gasps of disbelief were heard throughout the courtroom. He had just committed a highly

Shown is the record of Susan B. Anthony's conviction in the Circuit Court of the United States, Northern District of New York.

unusual act. He had instructed the jury to find Susan B. Anthony guilty. The jury's job in a criminal case is to discuss privately the facts in the defendant's case, and then decide, based on the facts alone, if the defendant is innocent or guilty. Once a verdict is reached, the jury tells the judge and the defendant its verdict. A judge is not supposed to decide the defendant's verdict in a criminal case. This denies the defendant's right to a trial by jury. (Unfortunately for Susan B. Anthony, Congress upheld Judge Hunt's actions.)

Anthony's attorney jumped up from his chair and protested Judge Hunt's actions: "That is a direction no Court has power to make in a criminal case."[14]

Judge Hunt ignored Selden and repeated his instruction that the jury should find Susan B. Anthony guilty. Selden tried again on Anthony's behalf, asking if each juror could be polled. This is a traditional court procedure to find out if any juror would make a last-minute verdict change. Instead, Judge Hunt again ignored Selden's request, discharged the jury, and closed the trial.

Judge Hunt never allowed the jury to discuss Anthony's case and never asked the jury for a verdict. In her diary, Anthony wrote her opinion of Judge Hunt's verdict and actions: "The greatest outrage History ever witnessed."[15] She added, "We were convicted before we had a hearing and the trial was a mere farce."[16]

The Sentencing

On the morning of June 18, Selden asked for a new trial so that the jury could issue its own verdict. Judge Hunt denied his request. He then ordered Anthony to stand. He asked if she wanted to say anything before she was sentenced. For a very brief time, all was silent in the courtroom. Then Anthony spoke clearly and forcefully:

> Yes, your honor, I have many things to say; for in your ordered verdict of guilty, you have trampled under foot every vital principle of our government. My natural rights, my civil rights, my political rights, my judicial rights, are all alike ignored. Robbed of the fundamental privilege of citizenship, I am degraded from the status of a citizen to that of a subject; and not only myself individually, but all of my sex, are, by your honor's verdict, doomed to political subjection under this, so-called, form of government.[17]

Judge Hunt tried to cut Anthony off. He told her he did not want to listen to the arguments that had already been presented during her trial.

Anthony continued,

> May it please your honor, I am not arguing the question, but simply stating the reasons why sentence cannot, in justice, be pronounced against me. Your denial of my citizen's right to vote, is the denial of my right of consent as one of the governed, the denial of my right of representation as one of the taxed, the denial of my right to a trial by a jury of my peers.[18]

"The Court cannot allow the prisoner to go on," Judge Hunt interrupted.[19]

Anthony smoothly continued:

> But your honor will not deny me this one and only poor privilege of protest against this high-handed outrage upon my citizen's rights. May it please the Court to remember that since the day of my arrest last November, this is the first

time that either myself or any person of my disfranchised class has been allowed a word of defense before judge or jury.[20]

Again Judge Hunt cut her off. "The prisoner must sit down—the Court cannot allow it."[21]

Anthony kept talking. She informed the crowded courtroom that every person who handled her case, including the judge and jury, were all males and they were all viewed as her political superiors. Judge Hunt interrupted once more, saying, "The prisoner has been tried according to the established forms of law."[22]

This point brought more words from Anthony:

Yes, your honor, but by forms of law all made by men, interpreted by men, administered by men, in favor of men, and against women; and hence, your honor's ordered verdict of guilty, against a United States citizen for the exercise of *'that citizen's right to vote,'* simply because that citizen was a woman and not a man. . . . Women [must] get their right to a voice in this government . . . and I have taken mine, and mean to take it at every possible opportunity.[23]

Judge Hunt ordered Anthony to be quiet and to sit down. Undaunted, Anthony pressed on.

When I was brought before your honor for trial, I hoped for a broad and liberal interpretation of the Constitution and its recent amendments. . . . But failing to get this justice— failing, even, to get a trial by a jury *not* of my peers—I ask not leniency at your hands—but rather the full rigors of the law.[24]

When Judge Hunt spoke again, Anthony sat down. Then the judge ordered her to stand to hear her sentence. Her sentence could be a fine of up to $500, prison for up to three years, or both. Judge Hunt sentenced Anthony to pay a fine of $100 plus court costs.

Anthony defied the judge by replying, "May it please your honor, I shall never pay a dollar of your unjust penalty."[25]

However, Judge Hunt got the final words. In the silent courtroom he said, "Madam, the Court will not order you committed [to prison] until the fine is paid."[26] Usually, the guilty person is put into prison until the fine is paid. If Susan B. Anthony had been jailed, she would have had grounds on which to challenge the verdict in the case. If Judge Hunt had put her in jail until she paid her fine, Anthony could have appealed her case to the Supreme Court, based on the claim that it was unlawful for her to be jailed. Now Judge Hunt had closed her case forever. The public, though, had plenty to say about Susan B. Anthony's trial. It was widely discussed in newspapers across the country.

chapter five

THE FIGHT CONTINUES

TURNING POINT—Of the more than one hundred women who tried to vote in 1872, Susan B. Anthony's voting case was the most famous. Her trial brought national attention to the issue of women's suffrage. The trial also marked a turning point for Susan B. Anthony. She now focused on getting a suffrage amendment passed through the U.S. Congress, instead of on a state-by-state basis.

Reaction to the Trial

Immediately after Susan B. Anthony's sentencing on June 18, 1873, reporters spoke to the jury members. Many jurors, they found out, said they were frustrated and angry with Judge Hunt and his actions. Further, many did not agree with his verdict. Other reporters raced out of the courthouse to telegraph news of the trial to their newspapers.

Judge Hunt's actions changed Susan B. Anthony's trial. No longer was the sole issue women's right to vote. It became a dual-issue case, the second issue being the constitutional right of a defendant to a trial by an impartial jury. Many newspapers nationwide, although not supportive of women's suffrage, spoke out against Judge Hunt and his improper actions in the courtroom.

The *New York Sun,* for example, said that Judge Hunt had violated a highly important part of the U.S. Constitution and should be removed from office. The right to a trial by jury also includes the right to a verdict by the jury, otherwise the jury is nothing more than twelve puppets manipulated by the judge, it wrote. Another newspaper, the *Utica Observer,* agreed with Judge Hunt's view of the Fourteenth Amendment, but said that he had violated the jury's power and in doing so had violated the rights of Anthony. The *Canandaigua Times* posed the question, If the proper legal duties of a jury are not enforced, such as in this case, then what could stop this offense from happening again?

The *Rochester Democrat and Chronicle* blasted Judge Hunt. The newspaper's editors called his actions a "grand over-reaching assumption of authority" by a man who believed "he is scarcely lower than the angels so far as personal power goes."[1] Another New York newspaper summed up the trial differently. That editor wrote that Susan B. Anthony "got the best of it. . . . Fining her one hundred dollars does not rub out the fact that fourteen women voted, and went home, and the world jogged on as before."[2]

Trial of the Three Registrars

On the afternoon of June 18, 1873, Susan B. Anthony attended the trial of the three Rochester registrars:

After her trial, Susan B. Anthony saw any publicity, positive or negative, as helpful to suffrage. This cartoon shows President Grover Cleveland, carrying a small book about women's clubs, being chased by Susan B. Anthony. Women's clubs were one place where women could learn about politics during the 1800s.

Beverly W. Jones, Edwin T. Marsh, and William B. Hall. A new jury was selected.

Richard Crowley was the federal government's district attorney and John Van Voorhis was the defense lawyer for all three men. The federal government had charged the men with the crime of allowing fourteen Rochester women—including Susan B. Anthony—to register and vote in a federal election. Voting by women was not permitted by the U.S. Constitution, said the government.

Judge Hunt committed various legal errors during this trial. For example, he refused to allow a supervisor of the federal elections to testify on advice he had given the registrars when Anthony had asked to register.

After the government and defense presented their witnesses, Van Voorhis stood to make his closing statement. This is standard legal procedure. Judge Hunt told Van Voorhis not to bother with his closing statement, saying, "I don't think there is anything upon which you can legitimately address the jury."[3] Judge Hunt then turned to the jury and told them that the women had no right to vote and that the registrars were wrong in allowing them to register and vote. He then told the jury to discuss the case and to find the three defendants guilty.

As instructed, the jury found the three men guilty. Van Voorhis asked for a new trial, but Judge Hunt refused. Each man on trial was fined $25 plus court costs. Edwin F. Marsh and William B. Hall refused to pay and eventually were put in prison on February 26, 1874. Anthony immediately went to the jail to see Marsh and Hall. She told the men to stay firm and that she would work to get them out of jail as soon as possible.

Anthony also sent an appeal to President Grant to ask for a pardon for the two men. During this time, the prisoners had hundreds of visitors, plus home-cooked meals prepared by the women they had registered. On March 2, 1874, President Grant pardoned the men and said that they did not have to pay their fines. Anthony was not pardoned because she had never gone to jail.

Anthony's Turning Point

Anthony's voting case was widely followed in the media, but when it ended in 1873, it still had not achieved widespread voting rights for women. Anthony looked to *Minor* v. *Happersett,* another case making its way to the U.S. Supreme Court. Perhaps this trial would have legal impact.

In 1872, Virginia Minor tried to register to vote in St. Louis, Missouri, but the registrar, Reese Happersett, said no. Virginia Minor sued Happersett. Her lawyer, Francis Minor, was also her husband. In 1875, the case reached the U.S. Supreme Court.

On March 29, 1875, all the justices on the Supreme Court ruled against Minor. They gave two reasons:

- Citizenship, under the U.S. Constitution and the Fourteenth and Fifteenth Amendments, meant only that people were members in a nation. It did not give anyone, including women, the right to vote.

- Each state had the right to decide who could or could not vote.

The case was closed and state constitutions barring women from voting remained in effect. Now Susan B. Anthony turned away from the idea of getting suffrage through the courts. Instead, she poured her efforts into her organization, the NWSA, with her focus on persuading Congress to give women the vote through an amendment to the U.S. Constitution. Meanwhile, the AWSA continued to work on getting the vote, state by state.

Continuing Work for Suffrage

Like other suffragists on campaigns and speaking tours, Susan B. Anthony was often subjected to physical violence and heckling, both in person and in the press. She continued her mission and, despite negative reaction by the public, the women's suffrage movement continued to take root and grow across the country.

Anthony worked tirelessly to educate lawmakers and the public, both men and women, about the importance of suffrage. She developed many methods to reach her audiences. For example, she gave cross-country tours, frequently spoke to the press, lobbied lawmakers, made speeches in Congress, and organized state suffrage campaigns. She also taught and guided other suffrage activists across the country. She was later called "an organizational genius," and it was noted that "her canvassing plan is still used today by grassroot and political organizations."[4]

The 1870s and 1880s were personally difficult years for Anthony. Devoted to her family, Anthony and her sister Mary nursed two of their ailing sisters and their mother. In spite of the loving, skilled nursing care they received, all three women died.

High Points

One of the high points for women's suffrage came in 1876. That year marked the centennial, or one hundredth birthday, of the United States. Philadelphia would host the first day of the Centennial Exposition, the country's largest celebration ever. That same year, the ninth annual NWSA convention began. NWSA members were frustrated at not getting the vote. They wondered what they could do to help educate the huge numbers of people who would attend the Centennial Exposition.

The NWSA decided to protest the lack of women's voting power during this event. After they formed a plan, Anthony and others traveled to Philadelphia to rent a place in May. They finally found something suitable downtown near the hotels, but only Anthony could sign the rental agreement. Under Pennsylvania law at that time, only single women could sign contracts. Anthony was the sole single female in her group.

NWSA members settled into their Philadelphia quarters and set up a suffragist library. They also held many meetings and receptions to inform the public about their cause. Anthony, NWSA President Matilda Joslyn Gage, and Elizabeth Cady Stanton reworked the Declaration of Sentiments that Stanton had written in 1848. They called their new document the Declaration of Rights of Women. They removed the old requests for equal education, the right to write and speak in public, and the right to earn a living. Women across the country had finally gained rights in these areas. Instead they wrote about the fact that the federal government was not a real republic because only men had full citizenship rights. Women wanted these rights, too, and could get them if they were allowed to vote. Once the Declaration of Rights of Women was completed, the remaining challenge was to get it included in the Fourth of July ceremony at Independence Hall.

Their request for fifty seats for the officers of the NWSA

during the opening ceremony was refused. Stanton then asked if she could present the declaration to the U.S. president. She was told that she was too late, since the program had already been decided on and printed. Anthony saved the day with a daring plan, which could have resulted in arrest and imprisonment if it had failed.

First, Anthony got a press pass through her brother's newspaper. Then, on the hot, muggy Fourth of July day, Anthony and four NWSA members sat in the press section of Independence Hall and listened as the Declaration of Independence was read to the crowds in the building. As the last words were heard, Anthony and the four other women stood up and quickly moved to the stage. Anthony led the way.

Michigan senator Thomas W. Ferry, acting vice president of the United States, was surprised to see Anthony. However, he listened to her short speech and, bowing low, took the rolled-up, ribbon-tied parchment copy of the Declaration of Rights of Women. With his actions, Ferry, a supporter of women's suffrage, had just included the women's declaration as part of this historic day. Anthony and the other women left the building, handing out copies of their document along the way. In an empty bandstand in front of Independence Hall, Anthony read the declaration to a large crowd. A five-hour meeting was then held to discuss the declaration. Newspaper reactions to the declaration varied from hostility to praise.

That summer, Anthony started a new project with Stanton—writing *The History of Woman Suffrage.* They worked side by side from heaps of old letters and

Some people thought that if women got the vote, they would behave like men. This 1901 photograph shows a woman dressed like a man and smoking (at this time, few women smoked). Further, the man is doing the laundry, which was a traditionally female chore.

newspaper articles. Together, the two friends spent ten years, on and off, working on this project and wrote three volumes. Three more volumes would be written eventually. The last volume, edited by Susan B. Anthony and Ida Husted Harper, was published in 1902.

The Traveler and the Speaker

Susan B. Anthony was a tireless promoter of women's rights. She traveled thousands of miles spreading her message across the United States. Starting just before the age of thirty, she maintained a rigorous suffrage campaign right up until her death at age eighty-six. Traveling by streetcar, stagecoach, wagon, carriage, horse, mule, ferryboat, ship, train, and sometimes on foot, she gave seventy-five to one hundred speeches a year for forty-five years.[5]

Anthony had been appearing in front of Congress every year since 1869 to raise awareness of the need for women's suffrage. To add more fuel to her congressional campaign, in 1877, she gathered petitions from twenty-six states, totaling ten thousand signatures. Congress did not react to the petitions. In 1878, she wrote a suffrage amendment that soon became known as the Anthony Amendment. If passed, it would become the Sixteenth Amendment to the U.S. Constitution.

It was Senator Arlen A. Sargent of California who stood before the Senate on January 10, 1878, and introduced the proposed Anthony Amendment. He read, "The right of citizens to vote, shall not be denied or abridged [changed] by the United States or by any State on account of sex."[6] Most men displayed indifference. Not until 1887 did the full Senate vote on this amendment, but it did not pass. The amendment continued to be reintroduced in every session of Congress for forty-two more years. Meanwhile, Anthony continued to speak each year at sessions of Congress until 1902.

As another way of putting pressure on Congress, Anthony made sure that the NWSA held its annual convention in Washington, D.C., every winter. She and the members called on and talked with congressmen and senators and testified before lawmaking committees. Anthony also organized and ran each annual suffrage convention, making sure everything went smoothly.

The International Suffrage Movement

In 1887, Anthony began organizing the International Council of Women to bring worldwide attention to suffrage and women's rights. To commemorate the fortieth anniversary of the Seneca Falls Convention, the council would meet for the first time in Washington, D.C., on March 25, 1888. Anthony opened the first session, one of many for the seven days. As she spoke, she saw delegates from

Delegates to the First International Council of Women, held in Washington, D.C., in 1888. Susan B. Anthony is seated in the first row, second from left.

England, France, Ireland, Norway, Denmark, Finland, India, Canada, and the United States in the audience. Over fifty organizations were represented. That evening, President Grover Cleveland and his wife hosted a reception for the delegates.

This successful event helped bring international attention to women's rights. The second council meeting was held in 1893 with twenty-seven countries represented. The third meeting was hosted in London in May 1899. Anthony crossed the Atlantic Ocean for the second time in her life to give the opening speech. Women came from all over the world, including the United States, Europe, China, India, Argentina, South Africa, and the Middle East.

Anthony was not content to fight for suffrage only in the United States. She wanted suffrage to spread throughout the world. In 1904, she founded the International Woman Suffrage Alliance. This organization helped focus international attention on suffrage.

By this time, Anthony had become an international symbol of women's suffrage and women's right. When she spoke at national and international events, she was honored and praised for her hard work and dedication. Anthony recalled, "Once I was the most hated and [despised] of women, now it seems as if everybody loves me."[7] Still, her mission was yet not accomplished—American women did not have the vote.

Joining Forces

By the late 1880s, women could vote in school and city elections in some places across the country. Only two states, Utah and Wyoming, had given women full voting rights. Something was needed to bring new life to the women's suffrage movement.

By his time, the NWSA and the AWSA had grown more alike. After many meetings, the two organizations merged in February 1890. The new group that emerged became known as the National American Woman Suffrage Association (NAWSA). Stanton and Anthony were both nominated to be president. Anthony, though, chose not to head the group. Stanton became president and Anthony was vice president.

The NAWSA worked to advance women's rights on both the federal and the state levels. After two years, Stanton left office to put her energy into issues of religion. Anthony took over as president and held this position until 1900. She emphasized the importance of gaining the support of organized labor (workers' organizations) for suffrage. Throughout the 1890s, Anthony also mentored many women. Two, she thought, held great political promise—Dr. Anna Shaw and Carrie Chapman Catt.

Shaw was first a teacher, then put herself through both theology school and medical school. Catt showed outstanding organizational skills, speaking abilities, and drive when she led victorious campaigns for women's voting rights in Colorado and Idaho. Anthony made her choice between the two women for the third NAWSA president when she retired in 1900 at the age of eighty. Anthony appointed Catt as president. By this time, only four states had granted women the right to vote: Colorado, Wyoming, Utah, and Idaho.

Catt quickly put together a plan to increase interest in the suffrage movement. She brought every state and territory into the NAWSA, even states without previous suffrage representation. She also increased the NAWSA membership, bringing

Carrie Chapman Catt, president of the National American Woman Suffrage Association (NAWSA), led the final march to women's suffrage.

many wealthy women into the organization. This helped money flow into the NAWSA, allowing the organization to better do its work. In 1904, Catt resigned for several reasons, including the ill health of her husband, who died a year later. Anthony then brought in Dr. Anna Shaw as the fourth president of the NAWSA.

Fighting to the End

In 1900, Susan B. Anthony suffered a stroke. Her doctors recommended that she stop traveling so much. As usual, Anthony ignored their advice and continued to travel around the country, giving speeches and lectures on suffrage.

Two years later, Anthony spoke for the last time before the Senate Select Committee on Woman Suffrage. That same year, on October 26, 1902, Anthony's close friend Elizabeth Cady Stanton died. Stanton had written of their friendship, "If there is one part of my life that gives me more satisfaction than any other, it is my friendship . . . with Susan B. Anthony."[8]

Anthony kept fighting for suffrage. She traveled from

"Failure is impossible!"

Susan B. Anthony continued to fight for suffrage right up until her death. Her final public words, "Failure is impossible!" became the rallying cry of suffragists.

Rochester, New York, to the West Coast, London, and Berlin. In January 1906, she made plans to attend the annual NAWSA convention in Baltimore, Maryland. She had missed only one meeting of this national suffrage organization and was determined not to miss another. By this time, though, Anthony was suffering from shortness of breath and dizzy spells.

In a raging blizzard, she left Rochester. She caught a cold but made it to the convention. She gave some speeches, then left for home. On February 15, on her eighty-sixth birthday, she traveled by train to Washington, D.C., for a celebration in her honor. When she stood at the podium to speak, the audience rose and applauded for over ten minutes. With Shaw helping her stand, Anthony made a short speech, thanking everyone for all their tributes to her. She also honored the hard of work of fellow suffragists. Anthony ended by exclaiming that suffrage would happen because "failure is impossible!"[9] These were her last public words.

Susan B. Anthony died on March 13, 1906, at her home in Rochester, New York, from complications of pneumonia. She was buried near her parents. Ten thousand people came to her funeral. Now it was up to other women to carry on the fight for the vote.

chapter six

MOVING TOWARD WOMEN'S RIGHTS

PROGRESS—Anna Shaw held her position as president of the NAWSA for eleven years. Under her presidency, the NAWSA made few gains in state suffrage changes. However, the NAWSA did grow as its image began to appeal to women from all walks of life.

The organization successfully recruited new types of members: middle-class, upper-class, and college-educated women all joined in. Working women, too, continued to join the movement. The NAWSA expanded its educational efforts by sponsoring debates and handing out literature to schools and libraries.

This building period for the NAWSA reflected major changes for many American women. More and more high school graduates were female. After their schooling, many worked at the ever-increasing office jobs now available to women. For families who could afford it, their daughters could go to coed or female-only colleges or universities.

By now, women could study for and get degrees in a wide variety of professions, including teaching, nursing, medicine, law, dentistry, and theology. By 1910, twenty-five percent of women aged fourteen or older were working.[1]

Sweeping Changes in the Suffrage Movement

Some women were not impressed with the slow-moving efforts of the NAWSA. When they looked at the voting gains women had made by 1913, they counted only a few. Just nine states had granted full voting power to women by then. Some other states allowed women to vote only on school, tax, or bond issues, or in city elections. Worse yet, the chances of passing a federal suffrage amendment seemed nonexistent.

Women tried a number of different strategies to gain the vote. Here, a group of women, representing different colleges, have formed a picket line in front of the White House.

Change was needed, and several American women accepted the challenge. Harriet Stanton Blatch (daughter of Elizabeth Cady Stanton), Alice Paul, and Lucy Burns had recently returned from England. There they had learned new, aggressive tactics while working with Emmeline Pankhurst and the militant suffrage group she had formed in England. Pankhurst was pressuring the English Parliament to pass women's suffrage. To raise public awareness of suffrage, Pankhurst's group held parades, went on hunger strikes, disrupted national sporting events, and did whatever they could to make front-page news.

Fired with enthusiasm from her experiences in England, Blatch founded the Women's Political Union (WPU) in 1907 in New York City. She came up with new ways to promote suffrage. Trolley campaigns, in which women rode trolleys speaking about suffrage and handing out literature, were run in several states. Blatch held open-air meetings, which had last been held thirty years before. One of the best-known WPU tactics was the practice of holding large yearly parades of women marching down New York City's Fifth Avenue. Yellow sashes and yellow banners adorned the marchers, and houses along the parade route sported yellow flags. Thousands of people watched the marches. Such activities were regularly reported in national newspapers and magazines and kept the public aware of the suffrage movement.

Paul and Burns took a different route. They disagreed with Blatch's state-by-state suffrage campaigns. Instead, they wanted a federal suffrage amendment to the

Constitution. The two joined the NAWSA in 1912, and with permission from the NAWSA's president, Shaw, Paul developed a big publicity plan to coincide with Woodrow Wilson's inauguration as president of the United States. The day before Wilson's ceremony, on March 3, 1913, Paul orchestrated a huge parade of eight thousand women, all marching for suffrage. Over half a million people lined the streets to watch the spectacular and unusual event. As a result, few people greeted Woodrow Wilson when he arrived at the Washington, D.C., train station that same day.

A month later, Paul and Burns formed the Congressional Union (CU), which eventually broke off from the NAWSA in 1914. Unlike the NAWSA, the CU focused solely on a federal suffrage amendment campaign. Members ran suffrage processions and parades, campaigned for petitions, and held hearings and public meetings. Delegations of CU members regularly talked to President Wilson and Congress about a federal amendment. In 1916, Paul renamed the CU the National Woman's Party (NWP).

In 1915, the NAWSA was infused with new life when Carrie Chapman Catt again became president. She soon developed a "Winning Plan" for suffrage. Under Catt's skilled leadership, the NAWSA encouraged and educated states in suffrage issues. Catt and the NAWSA also worked hard to convince President Wilson to support suffrage, since a suffrage amendment to the U.S. Constitution would require the president's support.

All these organizations helped promote suffrage. By 1917, eleven states had granted full voting powers to women. That year, a final push came for suffrage when the United States joined the fighting in World War I (1914–1918).

Getting Closer

During World War I, women joined the workforce in record numbers. They worked in jobs once held only by men. They carried their lunch pails to industries such as oil refineries, steel mills, and brass and copper smelteries. They took trolleys and streetcars to public service jobs such as governmental positions. Some women drove ambulances,

The National Woman's Party was formed in 1916. Here, members of the NWP hold a banner with a quotation from Susan B. Anthony.

others helped produce chemicals, fertilizers, weapons, and other military equipment. The hard work that women contributed during the war effort made it more difficult to continue to deny them the vote.

Catt continued to talk with President Wilson, to convince him of the need for suffrage. Under Catt's leadership, the NAWSA supported the war effort and put the vast majority of its efforts into that instead of running suffrage campaigns. NAWSA members helped staff and run hospitals, worked as Red Cross volunteers, and sold bonds to raise money for the war.

Paul and Burns took a different path. Paul, a Quaker, did not support the war and instead focused on suffrage. In January 1917, Paul and Burns began to place suffrage picketers in front of the White House. The women carried signs and banners asking for the vote. By June, the government began to arrest the picketers. Paul was arrested on October 20 for picketing and jailed for seven months. While in jail, she and other WPU picketers were beaten and force-fed when they tried to go on hunger strikes.

Victory!

News of the jailed picketers hit the national newspapers. With the publicity tactics of the WPU, the hard work of the NAWSA, and the rapidly changing economic and social positions of women, the time finally seemed right for a suffrage amendment to be added to the U.S. Constitution. On January 9, 1918, President Wilson announced that he favored women's suffrage. The next day, the required

Large suffragist parades like this one were popular by the late 1800s and early 1900s.

two-thirds majority in the House of Representatives voted to pass a suffrage amendment. It was a close call, with 274 representatives in favor and 136 against. Newspapers ran front-page articles on this exciting news.

It took all of 1918, half of 1919, and the election of a new Congress to convince the Senate to pass the amendment. To put pressure on Congress, the NWP staged demonstrations and pickets near the White House. Again, some protestors were arrested and jailed. Meanwhile, NAWSA members continued their educational campaigns. The NAWSA's work paid off. On May 20, 1919, President Wilson called the sixty-sixth Congress into a special session to ask for the passage of the Anthony Amendment. On June 4, 1919, the Senate, too, finally voted to pass the amendment.

One more fight was yet to be waged before the amendment could become law—thirty-six states, or three fourths of the states, had to approve the amendment. The suffrage organizations now worked together, and by August 1920, only one more state needed to approve the amendment. The spotlight turned to Tennessee, where a legislative vote was scheduled for August 26, 1920. The Tennessee Senate approved the amendment on August 13. National attention turned to the Tennessee House of Representatives.

On August 18, the Tennessee House was set to vote. House representatives wore yellow roses in their buttonholes to signal a vote for suffrage. Antisuffragists wore red roses. It looked like the suffragists needed one more vote to win, but where would that vote come from? Harry Burn, the youngest lawmaker in the House, wore a red rose, but he had a folded letter from his mother in his pocket.

Mrs. Febb King Ensminger Burn had written her son: "Hurrah! And vote for suffrage and don't keep them in doubt. . . . Don't forget to be a good boy and help Mrs. Catt put 'Rat' in Ratification."[2] When the House members voted, Burn called out, "Aye!" and voted to ratify the amendment. The entire House chamber broke into cheers and song.

After the governor of Tennessee signed the ratification certificate, he sent it by registered mail to Washington, D.C., where the secretary of state's office received it on August 26, 1920. After certifying it to be correct, Secretary of State Bainbridge Colby signed the Proclamation of the Women's

Victory! The Nineteenth Amendment is passed! Alice Paul, president of the National Woman's Party, is standing in the balcony with an unfurled women's suffrage flag.

Suffrage Amendment to the U.S. Constitution, and the Nineteenth Amendment became law in the United States. About 52 percent of the population, or 26 million American women, now had the right to vote.[3]

Immediate Ramifications

American women had won the right to vote, but they still did not have full rights as citizens. The law still treated women differently from men in many situations. For example, women could not be on juries, run for or hold political office, or will property. Men also received more pay for the same work.

To tackle these issues, in 1920, the NAWSA evolved into a new organization, the League of Women Voters (LWV). It focused on getting women out to vote, learning about the political process and leadership, and freeing women from legal discrimination. The LWV set up citizenship schools to show women how to mark ballots. Just before the presidential election of 1920, the LWV telephoned women to remind them to vote.

Alice Paul and the NWP approached these issues by lobbying for another amendment that would give full equality to women. They called it the Equal Rights Amendment (ERA). It was introduced into the House of Representatives and the Senate in December 1923, but it did not pass. It was finally passed by Congress on March 22, 1972, but since it has never been ratified by three fourths of the states as required, this amendment is not law.

Women's Rights Gains

After 1920, women started to make some progress in politics and in the workforce. Women took a while to understand how the political system worked. At first, women generally voted in smaller numbers than men, and many married women voted as their husbands voted. They tended not to rally behind women candidates or women's issues. Men still far outnumbered women in political office, as business owners, and in many professions such as medicine, law, and dentistry.

From 1920 to 1940, about 25 percent of married women worked outside the home, and the rest worked as homemakers.[4] That changed dramatically once the United

States entered World War II (1939–1945) in 1941. By the 1960s, women began to demand more rights.

Headed by Eleanor Roosevelt, the President's Commission on the Status of Women was established in 1961. The commission successfully pushed for passage in 1963 of the Equal Pay Act. It was the first federal law to require equal pay for men and women in federal jobs. It was the first of a number of federal laws that helped remove discrimination against women in the workplace. The next major change for women was the 1964 Civil Rights Act. This law prohibits job discrimination on the basis of sex or race. It also established the Equal Employment Opportunity Commission to deal with discrimination claims.

The year 1972 marked a major victory for women with Title IX of the Education Act. This granted women equal access to higher education and professional schools. As a result, enrollment of women in professional and graduate schools previously restricted to them soared. Women entered the fields of medicine, law, engineering, architecture, dentistry, and professional sports in increasing numbers.

During the 1980s, more women than ever before were in new types of jobs. America now had female Supreme Court justices, astronauts, arctic explorers, military officers, truck drivers, carpenters, bishops, and rabbis. Women entered other previously male-dominated jobs such as bus drivers, veterinarians, airline pilots, and phone installers. Today, women are working in nearly every field.

During the 1990s, a third wave of the women's movement evolved. More complex issues surfaced, and women

Suffragists Elizabeth Cady Stanton, Susan B. Anthony, and Lucretia Mott are honored as a wreath is placed on their statue in the U.S. Capitol in 1929.

continued to try to sort out controversial issues that greatly affect them. Some of these issues included women's service in active combat, women's leadership roles in religious worship, pornography involving women, sexual harassment, surrogate mothers, gun control, health-care reform, and protection of Social Security.

The Voting Power of Women

Since the 1980s, American women have become more and more involved in politics, as evidenced by these facts:

- In 1980, for the first time, female voters outnumbered male voters in presidential elections. This trend has continued to hold true.

- Female voters have outnumbered male voters in nonpresidential elections since 1986.

- Millions more women than men register to vote in elections each year.[5]

- There are more women than men of voting age.[6]

- Since 1980, a "women's vote" has emerged. Women, in general, are voting differently from men on some political issues. Polls show that women are more likely than men to vote against spending for military equipment and nuclear weapons and in favor of federal support for human services. Women generally vote more often for Democratic candidates and policies than for Republican candidates and policies.[7] Women are more likely to say they are Democrats compared to men.[8]

Such facts indicate that women could influence many elections. Yet female voters have not always voted for female candidates, even for those with similar views. Some women still vote the way their husbands do. However, female voting power has made candidates pay attention to issues of particular interest to women such as domestic violence, sexual assault, equal pay and job equality, and abortion.

Women are also gaining influence in public office. Since 1980, the number of women lawmakers and women in elected statewide positions has more than doubled. Women have tripled their positions in city halls. And women have moved from city councils, state legislatures, and county courts to Congress, the Cabinet, and the Supreme Court. The number of women in appointed federal judgeships and in Congress continues to grow.

In 1992, called "the Year of the Woman," more women were elected to public office than in any other year. That same year, women voted in record numbers for the presidential election. Women gave Bill Clinton the winning edge for the U.S. presidency in 1992 and 1996.

The Susan B. Anthony dollar coin, first minted in 1979, honored this pioneer for women's rights.

Because of the presence of more women in public office, women's increased knowledge of politics, and more women voters, an increasing number of bills on issues relating to women and families have been passed. The 1990s saw dozens of new laws go into effect that touched women's lives. Perhaps the most significant was the Family and Medical Leave Act. This law requires employers to provide up to twelve weeks of unpaid leave for employees who need to care for children or seriously ill family members. Since 1990, members of Congress have made sure that money goes to research on breast cancer. This disease is a leading killer of women in the United States.

The United States has never had a female president. In 1984, Walter F. Mondale ran for president and chose Geraldine Ferraro as his running mate. Ferraro was the first female candidate for vice president. Although they lost the election, this marked a first in American political history. Other countries have had female leaders, including:

- Margaret Thatcher of Great Britain

- Golda Meir of Israel

- Mary Robinson of Ireland

- Gro Harlem Brundtland of Norway.

Making a Difference

Susan B. Anthony's hard work and focus on suffrage helped pave the way for the passage of the Nineteenth Amendment to the Constitution in 1920, which gave women the right to vote. Since then, American women have continued to fight for and gain many personal rights and freedoms.

From an initial position of powerlessness, women, using nonviolent methods, have increased their rights significantly. The right to vote, coupled with women's ever-expanding political knowledge and influence, has helped women gain many personal freedoms and opportunities that did not exist during Susan B. Anthony's time.

As Susan B. Anthony foresaw, voting equalizes all of us. Each U.S. citizen aged eighteen or older has one vote. With that vote, each person can affect decisions about things like jobs, taxes, health care, and education. Voting affects our communities, our work, and our homes. With our right to vote, we can help to protect the gains of the past, solve the problems of today, and prepare for the future.

Questions for Discussion

1. Defendants do not have to testify during their trial. Would it have been a good idea for Susan B. Anthony to testify? Why or why not?

2. Compared to newspapers, what are the advantages that radio, television, and the Internet offer to people who follow trials?

3. Why do you think Judge Hunt prearranged Susan B. Anthony's verdict?

4. There were many leaders of the women's rights movement during the 1800s, including Lucretia Mott, Lucy Stone, Matilda Joslyn Gage, and Elizabeth Cady Stanton. Susan B. Anthony has remained the most popular and well-known leader of this movement. Why do you think this is true?

5. Susan B. Anthony led a nonviolent revolution in America: the seventy-two-year struggle for women's right to vote. Can you think of anyone else who has led a nonviolent revolution in this country?

6. Susan B. Anthony stood up for what she believed in, despite the fact that many people did not accept her beliefs. Has there ever been a time in your life when you

stood up for something unpopular? Discuss what happened and how it made you feel.

7. Susan B. Anthony had a vision (a goal) and a mission (a plan) for something positive, and she did what it took to accomplish her goals. She wanted to change things for the better for women. Can you think of anyone else who has done as much for positive change?

8. Who do you think is the most influential woman of your time?

9. What public figure(s) do you think has done the most for women's rights recently (1980s to the present)? How did you make your choice(s)?

10. The number of American people who vote has been declining since 1960. Can you suggest some ways to increase voter turnout and encourage family members, friends, and others eighteen or older to vote?

Chapter Notes

Chapter 1. To Vote or Not to Vote?

1. Ken Burns, "Our Big Time," *American Heritage,* November 1999, p. 101.

2. "Answers to FAQs," *Stanton and Anthony Papers Project Online,* April 4, 2000, <http://ecssba.rutgers.edu/ faqansw.html> (July 24, 2001).

3. Lynn Sherr, *Failure Is Impossible: Susan B. Anthony in Her Own Words* (New York: Times Books, 1995), p. xix.

4. "Susan B. Anthony," 2000, <http://www.trillium-graphics.com/susanba.html> (July 24, 2001).

5. Geoffrey C. Ward and Ken Burns, *Not for Ourselves Alone: The Story of Elizabeth Cady Stanton and Susan B. Anthony* (New York: Alfred A. Knopf, 1999), p. 38.

6. Susan B. Anthony, in "Arguments of the Woman-Suffrage Delegates Before the Committee on the Judiciary of the United States Senate," January 23, 1880, 47th Congress, 1st Session, p. 16.

7. "Answers to FAQs."

Chapter 2. Suffrage History Through 1872

1. Virginia K. Bartlett, *Keeping House: Women's Lives in Western Pennsylvania, 1790–1850* (Pittsburgh, Pa.: Historical Society of Western Pennsylvania, 1994), p. 141.

2. Elizabeth Cady Stanton, *Eighty Years & More: Reminiscences 1815–1897* (New York: Schocken Books, 1971), p. 165.

3. "Answers to FAQs," *Stanton and Anthony Papers Project Online,* April 4, 2000, <http://ecssba.rutgers.edu/ faqansw.htm> (July 24, 2001).

4. Geoffrey C. Ward and Ken Burns, *Not for Ourselves Alone: The Story of Elizabeth Cady Stanton and Susan B. Anthony* (New York: Alfred A. Knopf, 1999), p. 101.

5. Alma Lutz, *Susan B. Anthony* (Boston: Beacon Press, 1959), p. 119.

6. Ward and Burns, p. 106.

Chapter 3. The Road to Court

1. Alma Lutz, *Susan B. Anthony* (Boston: Beacon Press, 1959), p. 198.

2. Kathleen Barry, *Susan B. Anthony: A Biography of a Singular Feminist* (New York: New York University Press, 1988), p. 233.

3. Ibid., p. 250.

4. Katharine Anthony, *Susan B. Anthony: Her Personal History and Her Era* (Garden City, N.Y.: Doubleday & Company, 1954), p. 278.

5. *United States* v. *Susan B. Anthony,* "Order to U.S. Marshall to Deliver Susan B. Anthony to County Jail," December 26, 1872, Exhibit B, National Archives Web site, control no. NRAN-21-NDNYCRIM-131-B, <http://www.nara.gov> (January 26, 2000).

6. Ibid.

7. Anthony, p. 280.

8. Geoffrey C. Ward and Ken Burns, *Not for Ourselves Alone: The Story of Elizabeth Cady Stanton and Susan B. Anthony* (New York: Alfred A. Knopf, 1999), p. 142.

9. "Snapshot Stories: Anthony's Illegal Vote," *Stanton and Anthony Papers Project Online,* April 4, 2000, <http://ecssba.rutgers.edu/tidbits/snapvote.html> (July 24, 2001).

10. Lutz, p. 200.

11. "Snapshot Stories: Anthony's Illegal Vote."

12. Lynn Sherr, *Failure Is Impossible: Susan B. Anthony*

in Her Own Words (New York: New York Times Books, 1995), p. 108.

13. Ward and Burns, p. 42.

14. Godfrey D. Lehman, "Susan B. Anthony Cast Her Ballot for Ulysses S. Grant," *American Heritage,* December 1985, pp. 24–31.

15. "Application for Writ of Habeas Corpus, by John Van Voorhis, on behalf of Susan B. Anthony, Rochester, N.Y.," January 10, 1873, National Archives Web site, control no. NRAN-21-NDNYCRIM-131-H, <http://www.nara.gov> (January 26, 2000).

16. "Snapshot Stories: Anthony's Illegal Vote."

17. Ward and Burns, p. 144.

Chapter 4. The Trial

1. *An Account of the Proceedings on the Trial of Susan B. Anthony, on the Charge of Illegal Voting, at the Presidential Election in November 1872* (New York: Daily Democrat and Chronicle Book Print, 1874), pp. 6–7.

2. Ibid., p. 8.

3. Ibid., p. 9.

4. Ibid.

5. Ibid.

6. Ibid.

7. Ibid., p. 16.

8. Ibid.

9. Ibid., pp. 12–13.

10. Ibid., p. 14.

11. Ibid., p. 17.

12. Katharine Anthony, *Susan B. Anthony: Her Personal History and Her Era* (Garden City, N.Y.: Doubleday & Company, 1954), p. 294.

13. *An Account of the Proceedings on the Trial of Susan B. Anthony, on the Charge of Illegal Voting, at the Presidential Election in November 1872,* pp. 67–68.

14. Ibid., p. 68.

15. Alma Lutz, *Susan B. Anthony* (Boston: Beacon Press, 1959), p. 211.

16. Geoffrey C. Ward and Ken Burns, *Not for Ourselves Alone: The Story of Elizabeth Cady Stanton and Susan B. Anthony* (New York: Alfred A. Knopf, 1999), p. 148.

17. *An Account of the Proceedings on the Trial of Susan B. Anthony, on the Charge of Illegal Voting, at the Presidential Election in November 1872,* p. 82.

18. Ibid.

19. Ibid.

20. Ibid.

21. Ibid.

22. Ibid., p. 83.

23. Ibid., p. 84.

24. Ibid.

25. Ibid.

26. Ibid., p. 85.

Chapter 5. The Fight Continues

1. Godfrey D. Lehman, "Susan B. Anthony Cast Her Ballot for Ulysses S. Grant," *American Heritage,* December 1985, pp. 24–31.

2. Lynn Sherr, *Failure Is Impossible: Susan B. Anthony in Her Own Words* (New York: New York Times Books, 1995), p. 117.

3. United States Circuit Court, Northern District of New York, *The United States of America* vs. *Beverly W. Jones, Edwin T. Marsh, and William B. Hall* (New York: Daily Democrat and Chronicle Book Print, 1874), p. 144.

4. "Susan Brownell Anthony," *Women in History Page,*

2000, <http://www.lkwdpl.org/wihohio/anth-sus.htm> (July 24, 2001).

5. Ibid.

6. Geoffrey C. Ward and Ken Burns, *Not for Ourselves Alone: The Story of Elizabeth Cady Stanton and Susan B. Anthony* (New York: Alfred A. Knopf, 1999), p. 155.

7. Ibid., p. 210.

8. Sherr, p. 173.

9. Ward and Burns, p. 212.

Chapter 6. Moving Toward Women's Rights

1. Marjorie Spruill Wheeler, ed., *One Woman, One Vote: Rediscovering the Woman Suffrage Movement* (Troutdale, Oreg.: NewSage Press, 1995), p. 159.

2. Eleanor Flexner, *Century of Struggle: The Woman's Rights Movement in the United States* (Cambridge, Mass.: Harvard University Press, 1975), p. 336.

3. The Commission on the Bicentennial of the United States Constitution, *1791–1991: The Bill of Rights and Beyond* (Washington, D.C.: United States Government Printing Office, 1991), p. 74.

4. Lois Scharf and Joan M. Jensen, *Decades of Discontent: The Women's Movement, 1920–1940* (Boston: Northeastern University Press, 1983), p. 6.

5. Mark Curnutte, "Women's Struggle for Vote Too Little Respected," *San Jose Mercury News,* August 25, 1995, <http://newslibrary.infini.net/si> (July 24, 2001).

6. Cynthia B. Costello, ed., *The American Woman 1999–2000* (New York: W.W. Norton and Co., 1998), p. 357.

7. Nancy Woloch, *Women and the American Experience: Volume Two from 1860* (New York: McGraw-Hill, Inc., 1994), pp. 572–573.

8. Janet A. Flammang, *Women's Political Voice: How Women Are Transforming the Practice and Study of Politics* (Philadelphia: Temple University Press, 1997), p. 125.

Glossary

amendment—A change or addition to the U.S. Constitution since it was first adopted in 1787. The first ten amendments are known as the Bill of Rights.

American Woman Suffrage Association (AWSA)—Group founded by Lucy Stone, Julia Ward Howe, and Henry Ward Beecher that worked for gradual adoption of women's suffrage on a state-by-state basis.

appeal—Asking a court to review its decision or to hold a new trial based on new evidence; or asking a court with greater authority to review the decision of a lower court.

Bill of Rights—The first ten amendments to the U.S. Constitution. They protect the rights of individuals.

Centennial Exposition—America's one hundredth birthday celebration, held in Philadelphia during the summer of 1876.

Civil War—The war between the Union (the North) and the Confederacy (the South) from 1861 to 1865.

Congress—A body of the federal government made up of representatives in the House of Representatives and the Senate. It has the power to make the country's laws and raise money for government use.

criminal case—A legal action started by a state or federal prosecutor asking for punishment of a person accused of a crime.

Declaration of Sentiments—A set of resolutions or specific requests passed by three hundred people attending the Seneca Falls Convention in New York in 1848.

defendant—A person on trial who is accused of a crime.

defense lawyer—A lawyer who acts on behalf of a defendant on trial.

Equal Rights Amendment (ERA)—A proposed amendment to the U.S. Constitution to ensure equal rights for men and women. It reads: "Equality of rights under the law shall not be denied or abridged by the United States or any state on account of sex." The National Women's Party began to lobby for this amendment right after the Nineteenth Amendment was passed in 1920. Congress passed the ERA in 1972, but it was not ratified by three quarters of the states as required, so the proposal died.

grand jury—A jury that investigates criminal complaints and decides whether someone should be formally charged with committing a crime.

House of Representatives—One of the two branches of the U.S. Congress, which makes laws.

indictment—A formal written accusation of a crime.

jury—A group of people who have sworn to decide the facts in a court case and to reach a fair verdict or decision.

League of Women Voters (LWV)—Formed by Carrie Chapman Catt as part of the NAWSA in 1919. It became independent a year later. Headquartered in New York City, this organization helps women and men learn about politics and voting.

National American Woman Suffrage Association (NAWSA)—Formed in 1890 with the merging of the National Woman Suffrage Association and the American Woman Suffrage Association. The group fought for suffrage on both a federal level, by supporting a constitutional amendment, and on a state-by-state basis.

National Woman Suffrage Association (NWSA)—A national prosuffrage organization that helped fight for the passage of the Nineteenth Amendment. Susan B. Anthony and Elizabeth Cady Stanton created it.

National Woman's Party (NWP)—A national prosuffrage organization formed by Alice Paul. It directed ongoing campaigns against the political party in power, then directly on the president in power, Woodrow Wilson.

Nineteenth Amendment—Ratified on August 18, 1920, this amendment to the U.S. Constitution gave women the right to vote in all elections.

petition—To make a formal written request.

prosecutor—A government official authorized to accuse and prosecute (bring to trial) someone who is believed to have committed a crime. Prosecutors are known by various names in different parts of the United States, such as district attorney, state's attorney, and people's attorney.

Quaker—A member of a Christian group founded in 1650. Quakers believe in nonviolence and equality between men and women.

ratify—To accept.

resolution—A specific request.

Senate—One of the two branches of the U.S. Congress, which makes laws.

Seneca Falls Convention—The first women's rights convention in the United States, held in Seneca Falls, New York, on July 19–20, 1848.

sentence—In criminal cases, the decision by a jury or judge assigning punishment to a convicted defendant.

suffrage—The right to vote.

Supreme Court—The highest court in the United States. It interprets laws and the U.S. Constitution. The Supreme Court has the power to decide whether a law is constitutional.

U.S. Constitution—The highest law in America. This document, which went into effect in 1787, covers the basic laws and principles on which America is governed.

Women's Political Union (WPU)—Harriet Stanton Blatch formed this national prosuffrage organization in January 1907.

writ of habeas corpus—A legal document that challenges the right of the government to put someone in jail.

Further Reading

Kendall, Martha E. *Susan B. Anthony: Voice for Women's Voting Rights*. Springfield, N.J.: Enslow Publishers, Inc., 1997.

Monroe, Judy. *The Nineteenth Amendment: Women's Right to Vote*. Springfield, N.J.: Enslow Publishers, Inc., 1998.

Sherr, Lynn. *Failure Is Impossible: Susan B. Anthony in Her Own Words*. New York: Times Books, 1995.

Stevens, Doris. *Jailed for Freedom: American Women Win the Vote*. Troutdale, Oreg.: NewSage Press, 1995.

Ward, Geoffrey C., and Ken Burns. *Not for Ourselves Alone: The Story of Elizabeth Cady Stanton and Susan B. Anthony*. New York: Alfred A. Knopf, 1999.

Wheeler, Marjorie Spruil, ed. *One Woman, One Vote: Resdiscovering the Woman Suffrage Movement*. Troutdale, Oreg.: NewSage Press, 1995.

Internet Addresses

The Elizabeth Cady Stanton & Susan B. Anthony Papers Project Online
   <http://ecssba.rutgers.edu/faqs.html>

"Susan B. Anthony, Defendant," American Treasures of the Library of Congress
   <http://lcweb.loc.gov/exhibits/treasures/trr005.html>

Women In History, "Susan Brownell Anthony"
   <http://www.lkwdpl.org/wihohio/anth-sus.htm>

Index